D0602208

The Golfer
and the Millionaire

The Golfer
and the Millionaire

It's About Having the Drive to Succeed

MARK FISHER

PRIMA PUBLISHING

PRIMA PUBLISHING and colophon are registered trademarks of Prima Communications, Inc.

First published by Cassell, an imprint of Cassell plc, London.

Author photo © 1998 by Robert Lalibertè

Library of Congress Cataloging-in-Publication Data

Fisher, Mark.
   The golfer and the millionaire: it's about having the drive to succeed / Mark Fisher.
     p. cm.
   ISBN 0-7615-1468-6
   1. Success—Psychological aspects. I. Title.
   BF637.S8F555 1998
813'.54—dc21   98-6034
                                            CIP

98 99 00 01 02 HH 10 9 8 7 6 5 4 3 2 1
Printed in the United States of America

How to Order
Single copies may be ordered from Prima Publishing, P.O. Box 1260BK, Rocklin, CA 95677; telephone (916) 632-4400. Quantity discounts are also available. On your letterhead, include information concerning the intended use of the books and the number of books you wish to purchase.

Visit us online at www.primapublishing.com

To Muktananda

Contents

CONTENTS

Acknowledgments

TO EVERYBODY AT Prima Publishing for their unfailing enthusiasm, especially Debra Venzke, senior editor, and Rosaleen Bertolino, copy editor, for their subtle and profound comments; publisher Ben Dominitz; and acquisitions editor Steven Martin.

To my agent Cathy Miller, the best in the trade.

To all my readers who like the Old Man and who help me come up with new adventures.

To my "partner" Deborah, who polished the manuscript with love and patience; to Jessica, a charming young lady who played backgammon with me every morning before I "went to work"; and to Julia, who understood that I needed my sleep in order to write—or rewrite!—even if she is only nine and a half weeks old.

The Golfer
and the Millionaire

I

In Which the Golfer Had Stopped Dreaming

ONCE THERE WAS a man who didn't believe in himself. Many times he wondered: Why am I like this? But he was never able to find the answer. Eventually he concluded: Well, maybe I was born this way . . .

Although he earned a decent living as a golf pro, he had never managed to fulfill his lifelong dream—qualifying for the P.G.A. tour. Instead he had to content himself with selling golf balls and giving lessons to members of an exclusive country club.

Dealing with people who had made a success of their lives on a daily basis heightened his own sense of failure. And yet, when he was younger, he had been absolutely certain that his name would one day stand alongside the greats of golf: Jack Nicklaus, Arnold Palmer, Tom Watson, Nick Faldo, Greg Norman, Fred Couples, Nick Price . . .

His brilliant performance in college had raised his hopes. But when the time came to qualify for the P.G.A., his skill, which had never let him down at school, seemed to abandon him completely, like rats deserting a sinking ship.

By the time he was thirty, he had given up hope. After all, so many people were telling him to be realistic, to stop living in a dream world and make a life for himself. He couldn't recall how many times his father had insinuated that he had no talent—at least for the P.G.A. tour. So when he accepted a job in a golf club, his dad was really pleased. First because he himself was working there as a bartender, and second because his son had a steady job with a steady income. What else could you wish for to be happy in life? "Kids," the golfer's mother would say, who was a bit concerned because he wasn't yet married. What was he waiting for?

Despite the fact that he was now like everybody else . . . well, *almost* like everybody else . . . a voice inside him, growing weaker day by day to be sure, kept murmuring that he did have what it takes to be a champion, that he'd had a run of bad luck, that only an unfortunate series of circumstances had prevented him from attaining his goal.

That, at least, was what he was thinking as he smashed ball after ball onto the club's driving range, framed by a rose-tinted evening sky. He lined up one ball after another, like an automaton, like a man possessed, three hundred, four hundred balls, always using his number-one wood. His mastery was evident—at least here on the driving range— as his club made perfect contact with the ball, drawing or fading shots at will, all well past the 250-yard marker. So many balls had settled at the edge of the field it looked like there had been a snowstorm.

Despite the hundreds of practice shots he had already hit that evening, and the hundreds of thousands in his career, he seemed never to tire of admiring a beautiful drive. First the sensation of powerful contact as the club head connected "right between the screws," then the tiny sphere soaring into the sky, followed by that magic instant when, at the height of its trajectory, it seemed to remain suspended for a fraction of a second, as if weightless, before beginning its descent to earth, hitting solid ground, and rolling along the fairway. He felt uplifted every time he saw a great shot, especially from the tee. It had something to do with power, certainly, but there was also a sense of freedom, as if he were flying through the air along with the ball, as if he were living the dream of all human beings to fly like a bird.

The feeling was there again as he blasted another drive, this one covering a phenomenal distance of over three hundred yards. It wasn't the first time he'd passed the three hundred mark, of course, but it was always a thrill.

His elation was short-lived, however. His thoughts were overshadowed by something that had bothered him for years: the way the spectacle of his own talent only served to increase the bitterness and frustration of his failure.

I can hit the ball three hundred yards, he thought for the thousandth time, and I can't even qualify for the tour.

Although he had sworn to stop competing, deep down he had never accepted losing and still found the whole thing incomprehensible. The only explanation he could come up with was that he had been born under an unlucky star.

The sun sank behind the line of trees on the horizon and Robert—that was the golfer's name—seemed to awaken suddenly, like a sleepwalker. His right hand, which was not gloved like the left, was hurting him. He'd hit too many balls, he was stiff and out of practice. When he'd been training for the tour he could hit a thousand balls a session without feeling the slightest ache or pain.

His hands were powerful yet supple and seemed to have a life of their own. Women seemed to like them, too, and Robert was attractive to women, no question about that. At six foot three, with broad shoulders, abundant blond hair, and blue eyes, he was a slightly larger, slightly younger version of Robert Redford. He received no end of compliments and propositions from his female students, to the occasional chagrin of the male club members who, although much wealthier, were generally far less attractive.

He noticed a blister on the inside of his right index finger. When he was younger he never got blisters. He pressed on it with his thumb. It didn't seem too bad. If he stopped hitting now it would probably disappear in a few hours. He frowned and shook his head. What was the point of practicing so long anyway? He'd given up on the circuit, hadn't he?

Yet something that day had made him start thinking about it again, feeling the way he did when his dream was still alive, when he could practice from dawn to dusk without ever getting tired, carried along by his passion. What he could not admit, even to himself, was that he was hanging onto these painful memories because he was in a state of shock.

That morning Clara, his girlfriend of three and a half years, tired of waiting for Robert to make a commitment and marry her or at least have a child with her, had decided it was over between them. He understood and even told her she could keep the apartment, although it had been his when they started seeing each other. Right now he was homeless. The thought of checking into a cheap hotel depressed him.

He used a towel to wipe his broad forehead, covered with sweat and marked by an unusual scar on the left side. He couldn't remember how he'd gotten the scar. All he knew was that he'd had it since childhood. He thought about it quite often, as if there was some kind of mystery associated with it, some important event he had forgotten, suppressed, precisely because it was so important.

But then he would shrug off the suspicion and tell himself that he must have gotten the scar playing some silly game of pirates or cowboys and Indians with his pals out in the backyard.

A young club attendant walked over. "You going to be hitting more balls, sir?" he asked.

Robert jumped, startled out of his reverie.

"No," he said after a moment. "You can start cleaning up. Put my bag away when you're done, will you?"

He leaned his driver against the bag, but it slipped and clattered to the ground. The young attendant, a cheerful redhead about fifteen years old, hurried over and picked it up, then pulled a rag out of his back pocket and wiped off the head. When he was done, he placed it in the bag with what seemed like reverential care.

Robert noticed the look of unconcealed admiration in the boy's eyes. To this boy, and to many of the other youngsters working at the club, all of them aspiring pros, Robert was a kind of hero, his clubs worthy of the veneration generally reserved for a warrior's weapons.

Robert smiled sadly. It was amazing how the kid's image of him differed from his own. An image he'd have to live with for the rest of his life, like being stuck in an elevator with the office bore.

He walked up to the boy, ruffled his hair affectionately, and slipped him a generous tip, something he rarely did since the practice of tipping was frowned on by the club management. The boy's eyes widened as he looked down and saw the twenty-dollar bill.

"No, really, sir, this isn't necessary . . ."

"That's okay, kid," Robert said on his way out. "Just remember—never stop dreaming!"

The boy watched him go, pocketed the money with a smile, climbed on his tractor, and set off to gather up the practice balls.

On his way through the clubhouse, Robert pulled off his glove and found he had another blister starting on his left hand. "Damn!" he muttered. "I'm really going soft!"

In the locker room he considered showering, then decided not to, even though he'd been perspiring quite heavily. What was the point of getting all smartened up? There was no one waiting for him, no one he had to impress. He'd take a shower later, once he got settled in a hotel. After all, he wouldn't have anything better to do, would he?

He opened his locker, extracted a black leather overnight bag, then headed for the exit. On his way out he passed the shoe attendant, Rolly, a good-natured fellow in his sixties, a permanent fixture at the club, whom everyone liked. Robert waved, then spotted the old-fashioned black telephone on Rolly's counter—the club's last gesture of defiance to the modern world. He hesitated, then decided what the hell, he might as well try to reach Clara at home. Home! As if he still had a home . . .

He let it ring twice but hung up before anyone answered. Then, almost mechanically, he dialed the first few digits of his parents' number, thinking maybe he'd ask if he could sleep over for a few days. This time he hung up before he finished dialing. Things had been strained between father and son for a long time now. The thought of moving back home was just too depressing.

Rolly, rag in hand, watched the discouraged pro head for the door. "Let me know if there's anything I can do!" he called after Robert.

"Sure will, Pop! Thanks."

He strode rapidly across the parking lot to his car, an old Riviera. Although he took pretty good care of it, the Riviera looked shoddy beside the Jags, BMWs, Porsches, Mercedes, and Rolls-Royces belonging to the club members. Of course he knew very well he shouldn't judge people by the kind of car they drove. Cars were superficial, material symbols. It was just that the aging Riviera was a visible reminder of his failure, like a fatal flaw in his personality, there for all to see. He hadn't had the courage or perseverance to do what he really wanted to do in life, and now he was being punished for it. And the sentence was horrible: hating himself for what he had become, and for what he would remain, for the rest of his life.

2

In Which the Golfer Meets an Extraordinary Person

HE CLIMBED INTO the Riviera, threw his black overnight bag on the passenger seat, and turned the key. The engine coughed a few times, then died. He waited ten seconds, tried again with no success, and swore under his breath. Not only was the damn car old, it wouldn't even get him from point A to point B!

A club member got into the car in the next space, a gleaming red Porsche convertible. He revved the engine with obvious pride, glancing at Robert as he slipped on a pair of chamois driving gloves.

Too embarrassed to try and start his car with the other guy sitting there watching him, Robert smiled and lit a cigarette. Not to be outdone, the owner of the Porsche pulled an enormous Monte Cristo out of his jacket pocket and lit up, too, sending a series of perfect smoke rings into the atmosphere.

"How you doing, Rob?" the guy called, chewing on his Havana.

Robert replied with customary politeness—he could not afford to offend a member.

"Just fine, Mr. Birk. Sure is a nice evening!"

His thoughts, however, ran something like: Rich bastard, thinks he has something to prove. Always showing off . . .

Birk confirmed Robert's estimation by shoving the Porsche into reverse, squealing out of the space, and burning rubber halfway to the front gate.

Stupid as it was, the incident seemed to be sending a message, the same message Robert had been hearing all day: He was a hopeless failure, a nobody, no good to anyone. It was spring, and yet his damn car wouldn't even start! He tried to be reasonable. Worse things could happen. Maybe the engine was flooded. It wouldn't be the first time. Just be patient.

"Life just gets better every day!" he sneered.

He sighed, reached into the overnight bag beside him, and pulled out a flask of whiskey. He took a long pull.

A couple of drags on the cigarette, another couple of shots of whiskey, and the flask was almost half empty. He tried the ignition again and this time the engine caught. The medicine must have worked . . .

He shoved a cassette into the tape deck, his favorite Rolling Stones compilation starting with "Time Is on My Side," one of his all-time favorites. But at that moment, having attained the ripe old age of thirty, he felt he had no time left at all.

He left the club grounds and cruised aimlessly for awhile, emptying the flask on the way. At one point he found himself approaching a location he had promised to avoid—his apartment, or rather *her* apartment. He slowed down as he drove past the building and saw a light go on in the living room. He would have given anything to be able to turn back the clock twenty-four hours, to be back in that apartment with Clara, home. But he had made a terrible mistake. Now it was too late.

He hadn't believed Clara when she said she loved him and wanted to spend her life with him. Maybe he didn't feel worthy of her love. How could a successful career woman like her, making twice as much money as he did, love a failure like him, someone who had given up on the most important thing in life—his dream?

Yet she continued to believe in him. In fact, she may have been the only person in the world who did. But they had met too late, when he was already disillusioned, convinced of his failure.

Clara had finally announced that, if he couldn't accept her love, it was because he didn't love her. That was why he refused to commit himself or start a family.

"I got what I deserve," Robert mumbled as the whiskey took effect. "Jus' what I deserve. All those doubts I had, this is where I end up. So many times I couldn't bring myself to do it, to say 'Yes, I really love you, Clara. I want to make a commitment. Let's get married and have kids . . .' I kept her hanging on until she realized her love would never be returned. That's typical me, Rob the slob, always choking under pressure, screwing up when the going gets tough."

He pressed on the accelerator. He had to get away from the apartment, from all those painful memories. He felt like driving fast and far, all night maybe. The Stones broke into "Let's Spend the Night Together," and he pumped up the volume. He didn't have anyone to spend the night with, at least not the person he wanted to spend it with. She made that very clear when she told him to get lost.

Well, he would get lost. There was a freeway ramp just ahead. He'd hit the highway and let her rip, see if the Riviera still had some guts.

"Perfect!" he cried, and swerved toward the ramp without a glance in the rearview, soliciting a chorus of blaring horns. He turned the volume up higher to drown them out, and floored it up the ramp. As he rounded the curve at the top he was plunged into a nightmare—a black stretch limo had just slammed on its brakes because the car in front of it had stopped abruptly.

"What the—" Robert yelled.

His reflexes dulled by alcohol, he applied the brakes rather late, and a collision seemed imminent when, without thinking, he spun his wheel hard to the right. The Riviera went into a 180-degree skid and slammed into the retaining wall. Robert's head hit the windshield hard, and he lost consciousness immediately.

"You can't always get what you want," wailed Mick Jagger—the tape player was still working. Cars on their way up the ramp screeched to a stop, causing a few fender benders. Drivers jumped out of their vehicles and gawked. One man started running, intending to pull Robert from the wreckage. He stopped dead in his tracks when the Riviera's engine exploded and a cloud of black smoke spewed out from under the hood. Everyone felt the heat and stepped back. The smoke soon filled the interior of the car, and flames could be seen licking under the engine. If no one got him out fast, Robert would suffocate.

The chauffeur of the limo, meanwhile, leaped out of the driver's seat and pulled open the rear passenger door. An elegantly dressed man emerged, at least seventy years old but in surprisingly good shape if his posture was any in-dication. He was of average height, very slim—almost skinny—with a face that appeared amazingly calm under the circumstances.

He seemed to be concentrating, sizing up the situation, de-ciding what had to be done. He seemed to make up his mind quickly and began heading straight for the burning vehicle.

The chauffeur shouted after him, "Hey, boss! What do you think you're doing?"

"If my time has come," the old man replied calmly, "there's nothing I can do to avoid it. If it hasn't, there's no reason to worry, is there?"

He turned his attention back to the smoldering car. A second explosion sent more flames shooting into the air. Instead of retreating, the old man sprinted toward the burning vehicle, to the astonishment of everyone looking on. He had no trouble with the door, snapped open Robert's seat belt, and with amazing physical strength for someone his size and age, pulled the golfer out of the car to the eerie strains of the Rolling Stones' "You Can't Always Get What You Want." Moments after Robert's rescue, an-other explosion turned what was left of the Riviera into an inferno.

The chauffeur helped his employer carry Robert to the limo. As they struggled with his limp body, the golfer groaned. He was coming to.

The old man gently touched Robert's shoulder. "You're going to be alright. We're taking you to the hospital. What's your name, son?"

Dazed as he was, the golfer managed to mutter, "Robert. Robert Turner." Then he fainted again.

* * *

"If you'd just sign right here . . ."

The golfer opened his eyes and found himself facing a smug-looking gentleman wearing gold-rimmed spectacles and an expensive dark suit. Robert blinked a few times to clear his head, then took the document and examined it with some surprise.

"I represent the owner of the limousine you almost collided with," the man said by way of explanation. Robert noticed the limo's chauffeur standing off by himself in a corner of the room, fiddling with his hat.

"Where is the owner of the limousine?" Robert asked, the events of the accident coming back to him.

"Oh, he just stepped out to make a few calls. Now this is a letter of intent stating that you accept the sum of thirty-five thousand dollars as ample compensation for any discomfort caused by the accident. In addition you agree never to instigate proceedings against my client or to claim any further compensation whatsoever."

"Thirty-five thousand dollars?"

"That's right."

"Are you from my insurance company?" Robert asked, his mind slightly muddled from the sedative they had given him.

"No, as I said, I represent my client, the owner of the limousine you were trying to avoid when your car hit the ramp."

The old man walked into the room. "Barney!" he said, surprised to see his lawyer at Robert's bedside. "What are you doing here?"

"Well, sir, I . . ."

"I called him, sir," the chauffeur admitted. "I thought that, for your protection and what with all these lawsuits you hear about . . ."

The lawyer's jaw tightened as the chauffeur uttered what amounted to a profanity in his vocabulary—the word *lawsuit*.

"Edgar," the lawyer snapped, with an admonitory glance, "if you don't mind, I think we can work this out among ourselves."

Turning back to Robert, he added, "The settlement we are offering is more than fair, don't you agree?"

Robert evidently did not agree. "I'm not signing anything now," he replied.

"I understand," Barney said smoothly, "you want to talk to your lawyer first, right?"

"I don't have a lawyer, and I don't want one."

"You want more money then, is that it? You realize you're playing a dangerous game? As it happens, you were inebriated when the accident took place."

"Listen, just leave me alone! I have no intention of suing the man who saved my life."

"Barney," the old man cut in, "I imagine our friend here is tired. Let's talk about this later on, okay?"

"Yes, sir, whatever you say."

The lawyer stuffed his papers into a briefcase and stalked out just as a doctor arrived with some excellent news—the tests he had performed had all come up negative. No concussion, no broken bones, just a few minor cuts and scrapes. It wasn't even necessary to keep Robert under observation—he could go home immediately.

"Wonderful!" the old man said, smiling benevolently. "All's well that ends well, as they say. Can I offer you a ride?"

Robert hesitated, not knowing quite what to think about this unusual personage. His face was so serene, so completely free of wrinkles, as if life had left no mark on him whatsoever. It was impossible to judge exactly how old he really was. Most remarkable of all were his eyes: very large, very blue, twinkling in what appeared to be permanent amusement. They were the eyes of a man who, although he had seen many things, had not become worn down or wearied by life's long journey. On the contrary, he seemed to regard everything and everyone with the fresh, curious gaze of a child. His entire being expressed a kind of tranquil contentment that Robert found fascinating and at the same time enviable.

"No, that's okay," he finally replied. "Thanks anyway."

"Oh, but I insist!" It seemed the old man was not going to take no for an answer. "It's no trouble at all, is it, Edgar?"

Edgar bobbed his head. "No, sir, no trouble at all."

"That's very nice of you, but . . . well, since this morning I don't really have a home to go back to. My girlfriend and I just broke up."

"Oh, I see." The old man nodded as if he understood, not wanting to embarrass Robert by asking a lot of personal questions. An image of Clara's lovely face formed in the golfer's mind, and he remained silently pensive.

"Well, in that case," the old man finally suggested, "why don't you spend a day or two with me? I have plenty of room."

Robert found the idea absurd. He'd only met the man an hour ago. And yet, he thought, maybe it was destiny. He was no longer welcome in his own apartment, but if one door had closed, it seemed another was being opened. And really, what did he have to lose? Spending the night alone

16

in a shabby hotel room was hardly something to look forward to.

"I . . . I wouldn't want to impose . . ."

"It'll be a pleasure. Edgar, help our new friend get his things together, would you? I'll just see if there's any more paperwork to take care of."

The chauffeur stuck his cap on his head, hurried over to the bedside, and helped Robert up.

"Who is he?" Robert asked Edgar once the older gentleman left the room.

Edgar smiled. "He's a very successful businessman, and the greatest boss I've ever had. Everyone just calls him 'the millionaire.'"

Robert repeated the words in his head, trying to get used to the strange appellation. Well, he thought, if that's what he wants to be called, why not? Maybe he liked to cultivate an air of mystery. The millionaire was certainly one of the most unique people Robert had ever met, and the next few days promised to be interesting.

* * *

A short time later they were all comfortably seated in the old man's sleek black limo, heading for the Hamptons.

The golfer remained silent and thoughtful for the first part of the journey, staring out the window at the passing scenery. The old man seemed to understand Robert's need to think things over, and also said nothing. Finally, Robert roused himself from his thoughts and turned to face the old man.

"I'm sorry that I'm not very good company," Robert apologized.

"Not at all. You've had a hard day," the millionaire replied kindly.

"Edgar tells me that you're a businessman. And obviously a good one," Robert patted the leather seat and smiled
ruefully, thinking of his own wrecked car.

"I've had many years of practice," the millionaire said
modestly. "May I ask what you do for a living, Robert?"

"If I tell you, you'll probably want me to get out at the
next light."

"Oh? Why is that? Are you a criminal trying to evade
justice?"

"No, nothing as exciting as that. I'm a failure, actually.
That's what I do for a living. I fail at what I do best, which
happens to be playing golf."

"Is that so? A golfer."

"A golf pro, at a country club. You know what they
say—if you can't do it, teach it!"

He smiled bitterly, then, in a sudden burst of confidence
because it is sometimes easier to talk to strangers, he added,
"I used to dream about playing the circuit, maybe even
winning a couple tournaments. Now I peddle golf balls. If
you can find a better definition of a failure I'd like to hear it."

The millionaire did not reply immediately. He appreci-
ated Robert's candor. Few people were so honest, especially
on first meeting.

"But you're still young. How old are you, if I may ask?"

"Thirty."

"Well, that is young, at least from where I'm sitting."

"For a businessman, maybe, or for a writer or an artist.
For a golfer it's old, believe me."

"But wasn't Greg Norman forty when he was named
golfer of the year?"

"The exception proves the rule. And Greg Norman is Greg Norman."

"And didn't Ben Crenshaw win the Masters at forty-three?"

"He won a few tournaments when he was younger, too."

"Well," the millionaire shrugged, "if you keep coming up with good reasons not to succeed, you aren't giving yourself much of a chance, are you?"

The golfer frowned, wondering if in fact he *had* given up on his dream a little too quickly, if he really was going out of his way to find excuses. On the other hand, he had to make a living somehow. The idea of continuing with his studies, not because he wanted to learn more but because he couldn't qualify for the circuit, had not appealed to him. He couldn't see himself living on borrowed money, which is what most golfers had to do until they made the pro tour. Besides, he would have felt uncomfortable letting Clara pay most of the bills. Even with his job as a golf pro she earned twice as much as him, a fact which he always found humiliating, despite the liberal ideas that he professed in public.

"Tell me, do you think you have the talent to succeed?" the millionaire asked.

Robert realized that the old man had spoken in the present tense, not in the past. Somehow that made a difference—as if, at least in one person's mind, there was still hope, even if that person happened to be an eccentric old millionaire.

"Without meaning to brag, I'd say that I do, yes."

"Well then, if you have the talent, why haven't you succeeded?"

It was a simple, perfectly logical question, which the golfer found difficult, if not impossible, to answer.

"I really don't know."

"Maybe it's because deep down you never believed you could."

"Making ends meet and trying to qualify for the circuit at the same time isn't easy," Robert objected.

"Neither is becoming a millionaire. One thing's true though: It might not be enough to believe you can be a millionaire to actually become one, but no millionaire ever became rich without the firm conviction that he or she would succeed one day, unless of course they were born into money. I'm sure the same applies to golf. The rules of success are consistent, no matter what your area of endeavor."

"You really think so?"

"I don't think so, I'm absolutely certain."

Before the golfer could ask any more questions, the limo pulled to a stop in front of an imposing wrought-iron gate, which was quickly opened by a security guard. The limousine drove through and continued up a long driveway, lined on both sides by antique lampposts.

They cruised past one residence, inhabited by the gardener and his wife, then past a second, larger one—the staff house—and finally came to a halt in front of a third, an immense mansion, apparently the millionaire's main residence, which was more like a castle than a house. Robert whistled in admiration.

"Now I understand why people call you the millionaire!"

"Oh well," the old man commented modestly, "the real signs of wealth are not the external ones."

The chauffeur hurried around to open the door, and the millionaire and Robert got out. "Thanks, Edgar," the old man said. "I don't suspect we'll be needing the car any more today."

"Sure, boss." Edgar climbed back into the car and headed for the garage. A butler was waiting at the main entrance.

"Good evening, sir."

"Evening, Henry. Could you show our guest to a room? He'll be staying with us for a day or two."

"Of course, sir."

The millionaire turned to Robert.

"Henry'll get you anything you need. That's his job, so don't be shy. And tomorrow we'll see if you have the talent to make it as a pro. In the meantime, you get a good night's rest."

3

In Which the Golfer Learns Why He Failed

RIGHT AFTER BREAKFAST, the millionaire led Robert through the French doors, across a terrace, and out onto his vast property. Judging by the way the old man was dressed—yellow Payne Stewart knickers and matching cardigan and cap—the golfer realized he had been serious the night before when he said he wanted to test Robert's skill.

"I don't have my clubs with me, or my shoes," Robert said.

The millionaire regarded the young man with an amused smile. "Well, we'll have to see what we can do about that."

They walked through an immense rose garden enclosed by a ten-foot-high cedar hedge and through an arched gate onto what appeared to be a private driving range with panels set in the grass indicating various distances. There was also a practice putting green with nine red flags and a practice sand trap. A little farther on Robert noticed the starting tee of a course, the first green marked by a yellow flag about four hundred yards distant.

"You didn't mention that you lived next to a golf course," Robert commented.

"No, I suppose I didn't . . ."

"I guess that's why you know so much about the game."

The millionaire shrugged and smiled mysteriously. A man dressed in overalls emerged from a small white wooden structure and strolled toward them.

"Hal," the millionaire said, "would you be kind enough to find our guest a pair of shoes? What size do you wear?"

"Ten."

"And what kind of clubs do you use?"

Robert told him.

"Shouldn't be a problem, sir," Hal said and shuffled back to his shed. A few minutes later, sporting a comfortable pair of black golfing brogues, his left hand gloved, Robert extracted a driver, identical to his own, from the bag Hal had given him and walked over to the driving range where the millionaire stood waiting. He placed a shiny new ball on Robert's tee, like a pro giving someone his first lesson.

"Okay," he said, "let's see what you can do. Hit a few balls for me."

Robert settled into his stance, shifted his weight until he was comfortable, raised his club, and smashed a 270-yard drive straight as an arrow down the middle of the range.

Without saying a word, the millionaire bent over, placed a second ball on the tee, and stood back to watch. Robert found the older man's scrutiny somewhat disconcerting, but said nothing and lined up his shot, which he hit as long and straight as the first.

"Okay, let's see a fade," the millionaire said, bending over to tee up another ball. The golfer obliged by hitting a perfect fade.

"Now a draw," the millionaire instructed, setting another ball in place. A few seconds later the ball sailed into the sky, forming a graceful arc toward the left.

"Another draw, please," the millionaire said, as if he wasn't completely satisfied with the first. The golfer hit another draw, slightly different from the first. The millionaire clucked his approval, apparently convinced that Robert had fine control from the tee. He pulled a pitching wedge from the bag and handed it over, taking the driver back in exchange.

"Aim for the hundred-yard panel, would you please."

Robert hit the approach shot straight at the panel, leaving it four or five yards short. This seemed to pique his pride and he immediately lined up another. This one landed only five feet to the right. A third rolled two or three feet past the panel, while the fourth, a perfect shot, actually bumped into the stake, causing Robert to smile with satisfaction.

"Good, very good," the millionaire commented. "Okay, let's try a few putts."

The two men strolled over to the practice green where Hal the attendant had left a large bag crammed with various types of putters. Robert found one identical to his own. The millionaire also selected a putter, walked onto the green, and placed a ball three feet from one of the yellow flags.

"Right, let's see what you can do."

Robert didn't think it was much of a test. He quickly lined up the shot, gave the ball a vigorous tap, and sent it straight into the cup.

The millionaire placed a second ball five feet from the cup. This time Robert took a little more care lining it up, but sank it just as easily. The millionaire placed a third ball slightly farther away, about seven feet this time, a respectable distance even for a pro. The golfer took his time, checking the lie of the green. There didn't seem to be much in the way of a rise or a curve, so he hit it straight. The ball veered very slightly to the left, caught the lip of the cup, curled around it once, and then dropped in "by the side door," as the saying goes.

The millionaire pursed his lips and nodded. "Just what I thought," he declared. "Now I understand why you didn't qualify for the circuit."

Robert, stung by the statement, stammered, "But I . . . I just sank three putts in a row! And I did pretty well on the driving range . . ."

"I know, I know," the older man replied. "You have talent, just as I thought. The problem is, you either don't believe in yourself or you can't manage your talent. Or both, which would be even worse! Unfortunately, talent alone is not enough."

"But I thought—"

"I know dozens of young men with incredible talent who have fallen by the wayside, while others with less talent, but with a firm belief in their own abilities, succeeded beyond their wildest dreams. The key is knowing how to get the most out of what you're given at birth."

"Well, I'm not so sure I agree. I mean . . ."

"That's why there are so many really first-class people who fail in life. They do extremely well in school, get a degree or two, then fall into some crack and disappear— you hear nothing more about them. Others muddle through school with mediocre grades but end up building spectacular careers and making a fortune."

Robert was deeply troubled by the millionaire's words, which had opened a wound he thought was healed. He was one of those who had fallen by the wayside. As a young golfer, still in college, he had had some spectacular successes. Then, when the time came to get out into the real world, to prove himself in the face of some real competition, he had failed miserably.

"I even think that having a lot of talent can sometimes be a handicap," the millionaire added.

"Sounds like a contradiction to me," Robert murmured.

"Not really, if you think about it. Talent is a little like an inheritance you receive from your parents. Often being handed a pile of money, being born with a silver spoon in your mouth as they say, kills all the qualities you need to succeed in the real world. A lot of millionaires I know were born poor. They had to struggle when they were young, they faced terrific obstacles. But it was precisely because they had to struggle so hard that they were able to mold their talent, their financial astuteness, into a razor-sharp instrument, and use it to achieve much more than someone who simply inherited a million bucks at birth."

"I think I'm beginning to understand what you mean."

The millionaire continued, "Of course talent is necessary, but it isn't enough. At school, someone with raw talent usually has an easy time winning. When he tries his luck against the pros and experiences failure for the first time, he isn't prepared, he can't deal with it. Often he falls apart completely. He hasn't learned to manage his talent and, more importantly, to develop those other qualities that are even more crucial when the going gets tough."

The millionaire paused for a moment to let his words sink in. Then he continued, "Say I deposit a million dollars in your bank account tomorrow . . ."

Robert grinned. "That would sure solve a lot of my problems!"

"Maybe," the millionaire said. "But would that make you a success? Would you be able to develop that capital into something of your own, make it grow? Or would you just sit on it, watch it stagnate, live off the interest you could get from someone else, someone who would really be doing something with it?"

"I don't know, I—"

"Your talent is like that million dollars. It just fell into your lap. Now you have to manage it, make it grow and prosper. Are you beginning to see now why you weren't successful on the circuit?"

Robert frowned. "Yeah, I think I do. And it's depressing me."

"On the contrary, you should be happy. Today is a big day for you. Why? Because the first step toward success is knowing what made you fail in the past. The cause of your failure is like a thorn that got stuck in your foot a long time ago—so long ago, in fact, that you thought it had become a part of you, part of your foot. You probably assume it was some character defect you inherited at birth. But when you realize that the thing that has been bothering you for years is really a thorn, and that you can get it out of your system, well . . . I'd say that's pretty good news, wouldn't you?"

"I guess so, if I can really get the damn thing out."

"That might be a lot easier than you think. All earthly activities—I mean careers, jobs, and so on—seem different from the outside. But for someone with a trained eye, someone who can see inward as well as outward, they are all more or less identical. They all have a single goal, a single purpose: to teach people how to control their minds. A Chinese sage named Lao Tze once said, 'He who dominates others is great, but he who dominates himself is greater still.' For such a man nothing is impossible. He can succeed at anything he chooses. If you want to become a great golfer, you have to learn to master your own mind. There are hundreds of players who can hit terrific shots under ordinary conditions. But when the competition gets tough, when the pressure gets really heavy, only those with discipline can avoid making mistakes. And it only takes one mistake to throw your whole game off track. All great golfers know that ninety percent of the game is mental. The same could be said about life: Both are just a state of mind."

Robert was speechless. Deep down, he knew the millionaire was absolutely right, yet everything he'd said sounded almost too simple to be true.

"Control my mind . . . but I already know how to do that."

"I don't think so. If you did you would have unshakable faith in yourself, both as a golfer and as a man. When you do become the master of your mind, you'll see the fruit of success even as you're planting its seed. Isn't the reason you resigned yourself to being a teacher instead of a player because you never really believed you could become a champion? If you had believed, would you have given up so soon?"

The golfer said nothing and the millionaire carried on, "Tell me something. When did you stop dreaming you could do it? When did you give up on yourself?"

"Three years ago."

"What happened exactly?"

"Oh, well, it was my last attempt to qualify for the circuit. I started off great, all I needed to get my card was a 72 on the last round. I shot a 34 on the front nine, so I thought it was in the bag. All I had to do was finish off the back nine with a 38 or less, and I had my card. I was so excited—for the first time in my life my dream was about to come true."

"And what happened?"

"Well, I had some bad luck."

"Bad luck?"

"I don't know if that's the right way to describe it. You can judge for yourself. On the tenth hole, a five-hundred-yard par five, I had a choice to make on my second shot—play safe, or go for the green, which was dangerous because it was protected by a small lake. On the other hand, if I made the green in two I was almost sure to end up with another birdie, so shooting a 38 would have been child's play from then on. I hesitated, knowing I'd have to hit a 225-yard wood from the fairway to get past the lake. If my ball fell in the water, I might bogey. Finally I decided to play it safe and go for par with an eight-iron. I was pulling the club out of my bag when I heard someone shouting from the gallery, 'No guts! No balls! He's gonna play it safe!'

"That made me mad. I just couldn't sit back and let someone call me a coward to my face. 'Watch this!' I shouted, and I told my caddy to pull out the three-wood. The guy in the gallery just grinned and said, 'You're gonna put it in the water.'

"Of course, he should have been thrown out for yelling at me like that, but there was nothing I could do to stop him.

"I hesitated, but by that time other spectators were shouting, 'Go for it! Go for it!' I couldn't turn back. I played the shot, hit the ball a little soft, straight into the lake. I felt totally humiliated, didn't even look at the guy who had dared me to make the shot. With the penalty, I was on the green in four, but I screwed up again—I took three putts to get the damn ball in the cup, which made it a double bogey.

"That was it as far as my card was concerned. I just lost it from that point on. Three bogeys on the next six holes. By the time I got hold of myself it was too late. I finished off with two birdies, but my final score was 73, one shot too many to get my card. One stupid shot. I felt sick."

"That's very interesting," the millionaire said.

"Interesting?" Robert exclaimed, trying to contain the sudden anger he felt. "I tell you how I destroyed my life and all you can say is you find it interesting?"

"Yes, it confirms what I was thinking a moment ago. You didn't lose because you lack talent, but because you lack control. If you had learned to control your mind, nothing that spectator said could have bothered you. As it turned out, you let your pride dictate your choice of clubs. Golf, like business, requires courage, no doubt about that. But you also have to know how to calculate your risks. In your case, you didn't absolutely need an eagle or even a birdie to qualify. So you took a needless risk by trying to make the green in two. A mental mistake, as you now see."

"No need to rub it in," Robert said. "I spend half my time thinking about it, about how I screwed up."

There was a brief silence, and then the millionaire added, "That spectator cast a spell on you."

"Cast a spell! What's that supposed to mean?"

"Well, in a way that's what he did. By predicting you'd end up in the water he was conditioning your mind, which is much the same as casting a spell. A lot of people do it. They might not know they're doing it, they might even have our best interests at heart. I'm always amazed at how little people understand the power of words. In your case, all it took was a few words from someone in the peanut gallery to destroy the dream of a lifetime."

Robert remained silent, thinking about what the millionaire had said. It was true, he had never fully realized how powerful words could be until now, until someone had taken the trouble to point it out, using an event from his own life as proof.

"I think you have a lot of promise," said the old man. "That's because, when I look at you, I don't only see who you are, I also see who you can become, and that person is very appealing. I know there's a great golfer in you. Problem is, you don't know it. You're asleep. The mirror you see yourself in is distorted. All you see is a failed golfer. That's who introduced himself to me in the limo. But as soon as you can see who you really are, as soon as you comprehend your own greatness, your life will be transformed forever."

Robert smiled, embarrassed. No one had ever spoken to him like that before. Not his parents or any of his teachers, not even a friend. No one except—he had to admit it— Clara. She had always believed in him, right from the start. She had believed in his talent and was even ready to support him while he tried to qualify for the pro circuit. But he'd destroyed all that.

"I wish I could've run into you sooner," said Robert.

"Really? Why? Don't you think we meet people exactly when we're supposed to meet them?"

"Maybe. I never really thought about it. What I mean is, I guess I feel it's too late for me."

"At thirty years old? Too late? You must be joking. You have your whole life ahead of you. You've got talent, as you just demonstrated. The only thing you don't know is how to manage it, how to make it work for you so you can benefit from it. Maybe all you need is to learn how to prepare yourself for a tournament. As the Chinese philosopher Sun Tzu said: 'A great warrior wins the battle even before confronting his enemy.' The same applies to a great golfer. He knows that a golf tournament is a battle, not so much against other golfers as against himself. And he prepares himself accordingly."

"It's been awhile since I gave up training seriously—since I gave up competing. I don't need much preparation to give lessons to amateurs with a twenty-five handicap."

"But before, when you still dreamed of making the pro tour, you must have had some special way of preparing yourself . . ."

"Yeah, sure, I guess so."

"Well, since we're on a practice green, why don't you show me?"

Robert shrugged, unsure about where all this was leading, wondering if it was all just an exercise in futility. On the other hand, he didn't have anything better to do with his time. Thursday happened to be his day off at work, so there was no problem there. If he were on his own he'd probably spend the day regretting his falling out with Clara. Looking for an apartment, maybe that's what he should be doing, since he had no place to live and could not count on the old millionaire's hospitality forever. He'd have to find his own place as soon as possible. And then there was his car, the Riviera, totaled in the accident. He'd have to find something to replace it.

The old man interrupted this rather gloomy train of thought. "Why don't you start your warm-up exercises? I'm just going to take a walk around. I'll be back in a few minutes."

"Okay, sure," Robert said, thinking, Ah, what the hell, I can take care of all that stuff later.

4

In Which the Golfer Learns the Right Way to Practice

BY THE TIME the millionaire returned to the practice green, Robert had already sunk more than fifty putts of varying distances. His attitude was one of amused nonchalance as the millionaire watched him for a few moments, saying nothing, standing a little ways off. Then the millionaire surprised Robert by suddenly striding over to a large oak tree, which cast its shadow over the green at certain times of day, and throwing darts at the trunk.

Robert waited to see what would happen next. Since the millionaire seemed to take no more notice of him, Robert tried a few more putts, then gave up and walked over to the tree.

"Would it be impolite to ask what you're doing?"

"The same thing as you," the millionaire replied.

"The same thing as me?"

"That's right. Exactly the same as you. I'm not practicing golf, and neither are you. Not really. Well actually, you were half practicing, but half a practice produces half the results. Not surprising that you didn't win more often."

"I'm not sure I understand."

"Alright, I'll try to explain. There are two ways to practice putting. The first, which was what you were doing, helps develop your touch, your feeling for distance, and so on. It's good training, but it's not enough. At least not if you hope to win any tournaments. Then there's the second way."

Without saying any more the millionaire abandoned his darts, leaving them stuck in the tree, walked over to the green, and picked up his own putter, which he had left lying on the fringe. Then he took a piece of chalk out of his pocket and drew a line from the cup, about a foot long. Robert assumed he was drawing the trajectory of a putt.

"Now," the millionaire said, "how can I make this line shorter without touching it?"

"I don't know," Robert replied after a moment's reflection, wondering what this little sleight of hand had to do with golf. The millionaire bent over and drew a second line beside the first, this one about two feet long. And in fact, when he had finished, the first line really did appear shorter.

"Neat trick," Robert admitted.

The millionaire used his putter to nudge a ball toward the cup, leaving it about three feet away. It was a straight putt, on a slight upward incline, an easy shot for someone of Robert's caliber, especially since the green was perfectly manicured. The millionaire bent over again and made a little chalk mark behind the ball. Then he stood up and said, "Here's another riddle. How can I make this putt seem longer without touching the ball?"

"Well," Robert said, "if I follow your reasoning about the two lines, all I have to do is . . ." Instead of finishing the sentence, he placed another ball a foot and a half from the cup. "There," he said, "now my putt seems longer than the one of my opponent, who hit a better approach shot."

"Very good," the millionaire conceded. "Although not quite what I had in mind."

He reached into his pocket and pulled out a thousand-dollar bill. "I'll bet you a thousand dollars you miss this putt."

Robert looked at the old man with a smile that expressed both surprise and amusement. "Listen," he said, "I make a living playing golf, even if I didn't qualify for the P.G.A. A three-foot putt, especially a straight one like this . . . well frankly, I could sink twenty in a row. I don't want to take your money. It may not mean much to you, but it's still money."

"I'm ready to wager if you are, as long as you give me a couple chances to win it back."

Although he didn't fully understand what the millionaire had in mind, Robert acquiesced.

"Well, if you insist."

He placed the head of his putter behind the ball and got into his stance, making sure there wasn't a hidden curve or drop between the ball and the cup. Seeing nothing of the kind, he couldn't help but smile, savoring victory—it would be the easiest thousand dollars he had ever made. He gave the ball a firm tap and it disappeared into the cup. Looking up, he said, "I warned you!"

The old man didn't bat an eye as he handed over the crisp thousand-dollar bill. Robert stuffed it into his pocket, congratulating himself on his good fortune. The millionaire used his putter to nudge another ball to the same mark.

"Now another wager. Ten thousand dollars says you miss the same putt."

"Ten thousand dollars?" Robert gulped. He couldn't go back on his word. He'd said he'd give the old man a chance to win his money back, hadn't he? What he hadn't considered was that the bet might be raised in multiples of ten.

Robert nervously lined up the shot, his brain racing: What if I miss? Where the hell am I going to get ten thousand dollars? No, I can't miss. I just sank the exact same putt. But it could happen. I've missed a few short ones before. I remember one that was only a foot and a half . . .

He did his utmost to clear his mind. There was no turning back now. He checked the line of the shot, told himself not to lift his head as he made contact with the ball, something that often happened in pressure situations. He repeated to himself that he had just made the same shot with no trouble at all, so there couldn't be any unpleasant surprises in store for him as was sometimes the case on a first try. Reassured, he was just about to make the shot when he thought of something else and looked up.

"Just one question. I hope you're not going to keep betting until you win, are you? Because, I mean, mathematically speaking, I'm bound to miss one sooner or later."

The millionaire laughed. "Not at all, I can assure you."

"Alright then . . ."

Robert took his time checking the lie of the green again, getting comfortable in his stance, shifting back and forth until his weight was spread evenly on both feet. Finally he swung the putter back in a perfect arc and—perhaps because he was impatient, or because he wanted to get it over with, or maybe because ten thousand dollars seemed like such a large sum of money—he lifted his head just before his club made contact. It was the slightest of movements, but it pulled the shot, sending the ball toward the left of the cup. For a moment Robert's heart was in his mouth. He was sure he'd missed. He watched the ball catch the left rim of the cup, complete a half circle around the edge, and come to rest on the right side. He could feel the blood pounding in his temples. Only then, as if pulled by the force of gravity, did the ball teeter and finally drop into the hole.

Robert exhaled in sweet relief. God! He'd almost missed, even though it was such an easy shot, almost a giveaway. He emitted a nervous laugh, which he immediately stifled, not wanting to gloat in any way, even though he was now ahead eleven thousand dollars. The millionaire counted the money off a roll of about twenty thousand-dollar bills, which he always carried around for spending money, and handed it over like the good sport he was, as if money meant nothing to him.

Finding it difficult to control the trembling in his hands, Robert folded the bills and pocketed them. He'd never had so much money at one time before in his life.

"One last wager, and then we'll stop. A hundred thousand dollars says you miss the same putt."

Without waiting for an answer, the millionaire scooped Robert's ball out of the hole and placed it on the chalk mark.

"A hundred thousand dollars?" Robert stammered.

"That's right," the millionaire said, cool as a cucumber.

Once again Robert's mind shifted into high gear. He swallowed a mouthful of saliva to wet his suddenly parched throat. A hundred thousand bucks! What an opportunity! But what if he missed? He'd never be able to pay. He'd have to work for the old guy for the next ten years!

In the final analysis, he realized he could not refuse. The decision was simple—he had to face the music. It was only a three-foot putt after all. He'd just sunk two in a row. Okay, he'd almost screwed up the second one by lifting his head at the last moment, but he wouldn't make the same mistake twice.

He got set in his stance, tried to shake some of the tension out of his legs and hands, and was about to swing the putter head back when he lost control. His nerves seemed to crumble as a voice in his head kept repeating: A hundred thousand dollars . . . a hundred thousand dollars . . . Beads of sweat dripped from his forehead. He realized he wasn't breathing—he'd been holding his breath for the last thirty seconds. He took a deep breath, hoping it would calm him down. A hundred thousand dollars! He could live on that for five years. He could also sign his life away for longer than that. He'd never be able to borrow from a bank, with his credit rating they'd laugh in his face. He heard the voice chanting the sum over and over in his mind like a litany.

Three feet, a simple little three-foot putt, and he'd be a hundred thousand dollars richer. His hands were trembling, his palms moist. He felt paralyzed with fear. It suddenly seemed that the shot wasn't as straight as it had looked before. Maybe he'd been lucky the first time. Maybe the millionaire knew something about the green he didn't. Maybe there was a secret curve built into it, which is why he'd almost missed his second shot.

He remembered a couple of other putts he'd missed, much the same as this one, some even shorter, and remembered how devastated he had felt. He had to get hold of himself. He couldn't just stand there forever. It was ridiculous agonizing like this over a three-foot putt. He also knew that the longer he put it off, the harder the shot would become. Fear was making his muscles stiffer by the second. His confidence had all but evaporated, and that was certain to have an effect on his judgment.

He guessed the old man was having a good laugh at his expense. God, he should just get it over with! He was making a mountain out of a molehill. He bent over, eyed the cup again, lifted the putter back. He was so nervous the putter head swung out instead of straight back. Robert had the good sense to abort the shot before making contact with the ball.

Shamefaced, he avoided eye contact with the millionaire, and tried to get hold of himself by stepping away from the ball and taking a few practice swings. His hands were still trembling, and a swarm of butterflies was having a party in his gut.

The millionaire was watching attentively. He refrained from making any comments, however, and his face revealed nothing of what he was thinking, although he knew perfectly well what Robert was going through. Something worse than fear or doubt had seized control of the young man's mind—the horrible certainty that he was going to miss. He was completely convinced of it now. The putt was going to cost him a hundred thousand bucks! He felt sick to his stomach; the pressure was actually giving him cramps. He had never felt so awful in his life.

Robert gazed at the cup, then at the ball, then at the cup again. His vision seemed to blur as the cup appeared farther and farther away, smaller and smaller . . .

The millionaire finally put an end to the golfer's suffering—he walked over to the ball and tapped it in with the back of his putter—resolving Robert's terrible and insurmountable dilemma.

"I believe you now understand how a putt can be made to appear longer without touching the ball."

Robert realized that the millionaire had been using the series of bets simply to prove a point. He hadn't really expected him to putt for a hundred thousand dollars.

"Do you also understand what I meant when I said you might as well throw darts instead of hitting golf balls?"

"I guess so. I wasn't really practicing because in a tournament a three-foot putt is a lot longer than it is here."

"Exactly. And when you have to make that three-foot putt to win your first tournament, or the U.S. Open for that matter, the pressure is going to be a hell of a lot more intense than it is for a friendly little bet. There's no way you'll be able to stay calm and in control if you don't take your practicing more seriously.

"One part of practicing concerns your body. That's what you've been doing. You condition your muscles so your stance is right, your swing is smooth, so you know how far you'll hit the ball with each club. It's necessary, of course—you can't hope to win without it—but it's not enough. When the time comes to play under pressure, you have to rely on another kind of practice, what I call the practice of the mind.

"It makes no difference whether you have to make a three-foot putt, or a five-foot putt, or a hundred-yard approach shot. In pressure situations, it's your mind that counts, not your body. The important thing is to be able to control your mind, as I said earlier."

"I see your point, but it's a little like the story of the chicken and the egg, isn't it? I mean, it's Catch-22. A kid is looking for his first job: Everyone tells him he needs experience, but he can't get any experience until he finds a job."

"That's right," the millionaire said. "Nothing can replace real hands-on experience. There's no way you can know what it's like out there in Augusta on a Sunday afternoon, on the eighteenth tee, up by one shot, until you've been there. That's why exercising your mind is so important. You can't transport yourself into a Masters tournament, but you can re-create what it feels like. You can imagine yourself under the same kind of pressure, facing a putt worth two hundred fifty thousand dollars, and even more than that, this putt is going to make you a champion for the first time. You have to use the power of your mind to recreate the people crowding around the green, to see your name up there at the top of the scoreboard, to actually feel the pressure as millions of TV viewers sit on the edge of their seats, hoping you'll either make or miss that shot. You have to realize that golf, although just a game, can also be, under certain circumstances, a matter of life and death. Great golfers know it. If you can't understand that, you'll never be able to control your mind under pressure."

"You're right. I never used my mind enough, never took the game seriously, I guess . . ."

"One day," the millionaire continued, "an amateur asked Jack Nicklaus if he ever played a round or two just for fun. Nicklaus's answer wouldn't surprise anyone who understands the psychology of a champion golfer. He said he never plays for fun, but always to win, even with friends. He also said he never made a shot, either on a course or on a practice range, without going through exactly the same routine, giving the shot his entire attention. Quite different from the way you were practicing earlier, wouldn't you agree?"

Robert had to concede the point.

"For Nicklaus, every shot is important. Now, I know it isn't easy to imagine the pressure a two-hundred-fifty-thousand-dollar putt involves . . ."

"No, I guess not. Even if my rational mind can conceive of it, I still know a practice putt isn't worth two hundred fifty thousand dollars, that if I miss my life won't fall apart."

"Well, maybe you should make yourself suffer a little. Greg Norman—the Great White Shark, as they call him—has a little trick. He arranges twenty-five balls in a circle about two feet from the cup and tries sink them all without missing. If he misses he has to start all over again. When he gets twenty-five in a row from two feet, he goes to three feet. He says on good days he can get to six feet. By the time he's working on the last putt of the six-foot circle he really wants to go home and have a shower. That means the pressure has risen somewhat. Not quite to the level of a Masters tournament, but it's pressure nonetheless. Try it, I think you'll find it helps. Norman says it's a great confidence booster. And to be a champion you have to think like one. Champions don't function like ordinary people. They are always striving, analyzing, questioning themselves. They notice details that other people overlook. In other words, they use their minds as well as their bodies to get the job done, knowing that, between two opponents of equal talent, the one with the stronger mind will win.

"I have many wealthy friends, I know dozens and dozens of millionaires, and it seems to me they all have two things in common: a passion to succeed and an almost obsessive attention to detail. Their minds are always alert. Other people spend half their lives in a kind of stupor, influenced by a steady stream of useless thoughts and ideas. They spend hundreds of hours every year vegetating in front of TV sets instead of asking themselves how they can improve their lives.

"Successful people are always eager to learn, to improve, to discover the secret principles and hidden rules that make

things work. They talk to people who are already successful, who can give them something, help them learn more.
They take nothing for granted. Successful people are not
afraid to throw an idea out the window, admit they were
wrong, and start over. To them, problems aren't obstacles,
they're opportunities. Problems stimulate their creativity,
feed their passion and perseverance.

"A friend recently invited me to come down and play
at the Indian Creek Club in Florida. Ray Floyd's a member
there. As we headed for the first tee, we saw Ray on the practice green, lining up a putt of about eight feet. Two hours
later we were on our way to the clubhouse and there was
Floyd, still practicing eight-foot putts. His caddy told us he
hadn't stopped once. Now I don't know what was going on
in Floyd's mind during those two hours, but I bet it wasn't
what you were thinking about when you were practicing."

"No, I guess not."

"Hemingway rewrote the first page of *The Old Man and
the Sea* sixty times. Edison performed ten thousand experi-
ments before hitting on the one that lit up the world. They
did the same thing, over and over and over again, trying to
discern the secret truths, the celestial laws that make all
things, including golf, a part of the divine order. At the
same time they sought to tame the Goddess of Fortune. I
remember a quote from Gary Player, who said: 'The more I
practice, the luckier I get!'

"These people are like alchemists in a laboratory—and a
driving range or a practice green is nothing more or less
than a golfer's laboratory—trying to transform lead into
gold by transforming their inner selves into champions.
That's what I call real passion and real practice—the practice
of the mind."

The millionaire fell silent. Robert, deeply moved by his words, said nothing.

"Well," the old man resumed, "practicing is fine, but we mustn't forget that golf is still a game. How about a little fun? What do you say we play nine holes together?"

Without waiting for an answer, the millionaire walked off toward the first tee. His step was much livelier than one would have expected from a man his age. In fact, he was so spry he looked like a teenager, all excited about playing his first real round of golf. Robert followed, trailed by Hal the caretaker, acting as caddie, who carried both bags slung over his shoulders.

"Doesn't seem to be many people around, does there?" Robert commented. "Don't you have to sign in anyway?"

The millionaire turned to the caretaker and smiled. "What do you think, Hal? Do we need to sign in this morning?"

Hal tried not to laugh. "No, sir, I don't think that'll be necessary."

Robert realized they were making fun of him, and he suddenly understood why.

"You own the course, don't you?"

"The course is mine, yes," the old man replied with a twinkle in his eye, "but that doesn't make the game mine. That's one of the reasons I like golf so much: It's always a challenge, as you will see."

Robert looked from the millionaire to the caretaker, both of them grinning like wolves in a sheep pen. This probably wasn't the first time the old man had lured one of his guests into a match!

5

In Which the Golfer Discovers Some of the Mysteries of Golf

THE MILLIONAIRE INVITED Robert to tee off first, but the younger man insisted his host do the honors. He watched closely, extremely curious to see whether the old man could play as well as he talked. The millionaire planted his tee and very carefully set a ball on it, as if the height were of the utmost importance. Then he stepped back and gazed into the distance, as if seeking a specific point on the fairway. When he was satisfied, he assumed his stance, concentrated for a moment, then with a perfectly fluid swing, made good contact with the ball, sending it soaring. The ball bounced down the center of the fairway and came to a stop at a distance that Robert judged to be about two hundred and twenty to two hundred and thirty yards, very respectable for a man of the millionaire's age.

"Nice shot," Robert commented.

"Thanks," the millionaire said, retrieving his tee.

Although Robert had in no way been humiliated by the little lesson on the practice green, his pride had been piqued, so that he was now intent on demonstrating just how good a golfer he really was. He hit a formidable drive, almost three hundred yards down the middle of the fairway.

"Very impressive," the millionaire said. "You must have had your Wheaties for breakfast!"

"Never miss a day!" Robert joked, looking around for his tee. He pocketed it and accompanied the millionaire down the fairway, admiring the older man's calm, benevolent face.

The millionaire didn't take much time to think about his next shot and hit a fine six-iron, placing his ball about ten feet from the flag.

"That was a beauty!" Robert said, truly impressed.

"Thanks again," the millionaire replied, without showing the least sign of elation, as if he hit shots just like it every day.

Robert walked over to his own ball, only a hundred yards from the sloping green, which was protected by a large trap. He chose a pitching wedge, hit the ball a little soft and ended up in the sand.

"Damn!" he cried, unable to mask his frustration.

"What happened?" the millionaire asked.

"I played it too soft."

"Yes, I can see that. But why?"

"Why? Oh, I don't know, I just made a bad shot, that's all."

"I'm afraid that won't do. You have to look deeper than that for an answer, otherwise you'll just keeping making 'bad shots,' as you call them. People who succeed, no matter what they happen to do, always look beyond appearances. They're never content with pat answers. Maybe that's why they're called 'self-made.' Or maybe we should call them 'self-thinking.' People who learn to think for themselves possess the key to success."

The millionaire paused for a moment, then continued. "Now think about it—make a real effort—and tell me, why did you miss that shot?"

Robert frowned as he tried to come up with a suitable response, then gave it up.

"I honestly can't say."

"Alright, let me help you. I think you just gave in to one of the dark states of the golfer."

"The dark states of the golfer?" Robert said, wondering if this was another of the old man's jokes.

"That's right, the dark states of the golfer. I said before that to become a great golfer you have to learn to control your mind. Well, from what I've seen, I would say that golfers' minds tend to fluctuate between two distinct and opposing states: the brilliant states of the golfer and the dark states. The more you cultivate the brilliant states, the more you can prevent yourself from failing before you start, and the more tournaments you'll win. Winning top-level competitions is difficult, I admit. But, in a way, winning is easy. All you have to do is train your mind, develop enough discipline to control your thoughts and emotions, so that you can always bring out the best in yourself and avoid those moments of doubt and fear. If you can manage to do that, winning becomes easy. Mastering the game of golf is nothing compared to mastering your own mind."

"This is certainly intriguing. What exactly are the dark states of the golfer?"

"Well, the dark states of the golfer, as I call them, are made up of all those negative habits, those old tendencies, often unconscious, that prevent you from making shots you know you can make. That's one of the reasons you play differently when you practice and when you're in a tournament. The dark states don't arise as frequently during practice. But pressure playing is different. That's when a whole army of doubts and fears rush at you. If you don't know how to handle them, the results can be catastrophic. Take your last shot for example: You hit a great drive, and then you did what so many golfers do—you let yourself get distracted by a feeling of pride. Result? You sent the ball right into the sand trap, even though the shot was relatively easy for someone with your ability."

"I admit I may not have been concentrating enough, but I don't see what pride has to do with it . . ."

"You may not, but I do. Without realizing it, that great tee shot flattered your pride and made you drop your guard. It also satisfied a mysterious hunger in you, a feeling that may be the reason so many millions of men and women around the world find golf so fascinating."

"You mean you figured it out?" Robert said, half in jest. "I've been playing for twenty years and I still have no idea what attracts so many people to the game. What do you mean by hunger?"

As usual the millionaire, perhaps in unconscious imitation of the great philosopher Socrates, answered Robert's question with another question.

"Have you ever noticed how most golfers describe a good shot?"

"No, can't say that I have."

"Well, they use the word *beautiful*. 'What a beauty!' or 'Wow, that's beautiful!' Of course you hear things like 'nice shot' or 'excellent shot,' too. But 'beautiful' is by far the most common adjective. That's why even pros feel flattered after making a great shot and let themselves get distracted. Everyone hungers for beauty."

"And after a good meal, you aren't hungry anymore. Is that what you mean?"

"Precisely," the millionaire said approvingly.

"Maybe that's why the guys who hit the longest drives are rarely the ones who win tournaments," Robert reflected.

"Right again! Hitting powerful drives feeds their pride, and in turn brings in a dark state. Power equals manliness. The Chinese call it *yang*, the masculine principle associated with the sky, abstraction, fire. Approach shots and putts are much more feminine, or *yin*, the concrete, earthly principle associated with water. If you think about it, a tee shot does have a lot to do with the sky. The ball is not placed on the ground, but is lifted on a tee. Drives fly high, and cover most of their distance in the air, free from the earth's imperfections. A putt, on the other hand, is the least abstract kind of shot; it rolls along solid ground, pushed this way and that by angles and bumps on the green. In that sense, you have much less control over your putts than over a drive, which can attain a kind of abstract perfection."

"I've noticed it myself. Really macho guys never make good golfers."

"Precisely—because the complete player, like the complete man, is perfectly balanced. The masculine and feminine principles both play important roles in the game of golf and must be kept in harmony. To become great, a golfer has to know how to use a driver, no doubt about that. But he also has to appreciate the more mysterious, unpredictable, and secret power of making a delicate putt or a beautiful approach shot."

"Yeah, I remember something Jack Nicklaus said," Robert remarked with growing enthusiasm. "He said, 'It's no good having a million-dollar driver if you've got a one-dollar putter.'"

"Exactly."

By now the two men had reached the green. Robert slid down the side of the trap, measured his shot and hit a passable wedge to within ten feet of the cup. The millionaire sank his putt for a birdie, while Robert missed his putt shot, leaving himself with a two-and-a-half-foot downhill putt, complicated by a hard curve to the right, for a bogey. Despite his best effort, he missed that, too, and had to settle for a double bogey. Needless to say, he was not in the best of moods as they headed for the second tee.

6

In Which the Golfer
Learns Not to Be
Influenced by Events

SHAKESPEARE WROTE A play called *All's Well That Ends Well*. Robert's day on the golf course was proving to be just the opposite. Although the second fairway was broad and devoid of traps, he sliced his drive way over to the right, into deep grass.

"What happened this time?" the millionaire asked. "You were hitting fine on the driving range."

"I don't know what's wrong with me. Just one of those days, I guess."

"I think not. You're slipping into the dark states of the golfer. You have to be firm, fight it off. Don't let yourself be influenced by exterior events, in this case your last shot. Instead of deciding how you are going to think, you're letting events dictate how you play."

"Listen, I'm only human. I started the round with a double bogey. I think it's normal to be a little upset."

"It may be normal, but that doesn't make it right. The golfer you want to be would not let the last hole influence him one bit, especially if it was badly played. You have to decide once and for all who's in control here. If you don't, you'll never win. Just one bad shot early on and your whole game will fall to pieces."

"You know, it's funny you mention that because one thing I've noticed about myself, if I get off to a bad start, it takes me three or four holes to recover."

"And that's how you lose tournaments. Those three or four holes make all the difference. Great golfers develop an uncanny ability to be totally present, to exist only in the present moment. They can be brilliant even though a moment before they were caught in one of the dark states. They concentrate totally on each shot and put their whole heart into what they're doing, no matter what happened on the previous hole. They become completely absorbed in the moment, because they know that it is only in the present that action has meaning. Whatever happened in the past—whether it was their last hole, their last round, or their last tournament—means nothing. They don't think about the future, since there's nothing they can do to change that either. After all, you can't play your third shot before your second!"

"That's something even the greatest golfer can't do!" Robert had to admit.

"And yet," the millionaire said, "how many golfers lose their head and make costly errors because they're so nervous about an important tournament, instead of concentrating on the shot at hand?"

"I know, it happens to me all the time."

The millionaire played a decent seven-iron but brought it up a little short, leaving the ball on the fringe of the green. Before Robert had a chance to make his shot, the millionaire continued.

"Imagine that you're in a very important tournament, and after fifteen holes you're four under par. If you hit a double bogey on the sixteenth . . ."

"I'd be very disappointed."

"Sure you'd be disappointed, but did that double bogey prevent you from playing the first fifteen holes well?"

"No."

"And does a double bogey on the first hole count more on your scorecard than one on the sixteenth hole?"

"I see what you mean. It's just that getting off to a bad start is more depressing. If I double bogey the sixteenth hole when I'm already four under par, I don't get as discouraged."

"Well, that is exactly what you have to learn not to do if you want to be a great golfer, a real champion. If you don't learn this, you won't make any real progress, because you'll always be influenced by a bad start. You might be two strokes up on the last day of the Masters, but if you start your round with a double bogey and let it get you down, you've already lost. You might as well give up right away, finishing the round would be a waste of time. You have to cultivate a sense of detachment, otherwise the dark states of the golfer will inevitably take over. You have to be able to observe your own game like a scorekeeper for whom a bogey is a bogey, nothing more or less, no matter when it happens. The scorecard doesn't care whether shots are important or not. Every stroke counts for one.

"How many times have you lost a match or a tournament and thought, If only I'd paid more attention to that two-foot putt, or If only I hadn't gotten angry, I could have saved a double bogey. I could have made an exceptional shot, I could have won . . . ? Great golfers treat each shot like impartial parents treat each of their children. They are perfect democrats, favoring none above the others, giving as much as they can without regard for talent or abilities."

"I'll do my best."

"A missed shot means nothing and should have no impact on the next one. Unfortunately, so many golfers react to a bad shot or a bad round like some businesspeople I know—they encounter an obstacle when they're starting out, fail, and never recover. And yet they often possess extraordinary abilities. Many were more gifted than I am. They had friends and connections in the right places and capital to work with. If I had thought like them—and I expressly use the word 'thought'—we wouldn't be here today, playing on my private course. I don't know how many times I overcame failure . . ."

"I wish I could do that," Robert said.

"You will, you will. But while you still have a hard time with your emotions, I'll teach you a trick. I call it the 'stop' method. It's quite simple, really. Observe your own thoughts before making a shot. Whenever you feel the dark states creeping in, whenever you see that highway robber lying in wait about to make off with your treasure—your confidence and peace of mind—say, 'Stop!' Talk to your thoughts as if you considered them minor nuisances, little tests of character. I always had complete confidence that I would eventually succeed, that I would attain my goals and become the person I wanted to be. Life is strange. When it realizes that we're not going to submit—no matter what obstacles it places in our path—when it sees that nothing can drain our determination and enthusiasm, then, like a lover finally giving in after a long courtship, it gives us everything we ask for."

"I see, but it sounds like it's a lot easier said than done."

"Well, it is easy to maintain a positive frame of mind when things are going well. Anyone can do that, although there are people who complain even then. The hard part is to act like a great golfer, a champion, and keep your mind on an even keel even when things are going badly. That's what I try to do in business. During hard times I always do two things: First I make sure to take whatever measures are necessary to solve the problem, and second I tell myself, 'Don't hurry, don't panic, don't let this get you down. There's plenty of time to be unhappy, so why not put it off until tomorrow?' And if things are still going badly the next day, I tell myself that I can wait still another day to be unhappy, that I'd be better off using my time to remedy the situation. Most often things straighten out before I've had time to get depressed! Remember that the only people who benefit from your worrying are doctors and psychiatrists. And the only thing you can really control in life is your own state of mind."

"I'll try to remember that, " Robert said.

"Great golfers are so detached they can evaluate each shot on a purely informational level, without getting in the least emotional. It's like their own bad shots are happening to someone else. In fact, that's how they see a bad shot—it always happens to someone else, because the person who hit the shot was not living up to his full potential. It's like someone else took over for a moment and made a mistake, let a dark state in. The amazing thing is that the more you learn to let the brilliant states shine through on the golf course, the more they will affect your whole life. People who are able to master one field of endeavor see their whole lives transformed. They react the same way to bad news, to professional setbacks or personal disappointments, as they do to a bad shot. Instead of complaining and getting depressed, they remain detached and perfectly balanced. They analyze the reasons for their mistake, take appropriate measures to correct the situation, and always try to do the best they can, confident that in the future they will reap the benefits of their actions."

"Well, I agree that being detached is a good thing. But there are still situations where it's hard not to get emotional. Some shots are more important than others. You can't help feeling nervous, no matter how hard you try to be rational. Emotions are a powerful thing . . ."

"And there lies one of the paradoxes of golf," the million-aire replied. "When you practice, you have to pretend each putt is worth two hundred fifty thousand dollars, that it's the one that's going to win you the U.S. Open. And when you're actually playing in a tournament you still have to pretend, only this time you imagine that even the most crucial putt is just another routine shot on the practice green. On the other hand, when you develop the ability to let the brilliant states shine through at all times, you'll realize that nothing in life, either on or off the golf course, is of any real importance."

"I had a hard time convincing myself of that when I was trying to qualify for the circuit. I remember I was so nervous, so afraid of missing my shot . . ."

"That may be because you've never experienced real fear. If you had, you would know that ultimately life, too, is just a game, that things are only as important as our mind makes them. And since we can learn to control our mind, we can also learn to stay balanced under any circumstances. As I said, that's the paradox, both in golf and in life. You have to practice as if each shot were a matter of life and death, and at the same time make that crucial putt or hit that crucial drive as if it were just another shot on the practice field, or as if you were playing a round with some friends on a Sunday afternoon."

The next hole was a long par five with a dog-leg right. The millionaire suggested that Robert take a chance and try to hit his tee shot over the trees, which was the only way to get to the green in two. The advice turned out not to be fortuitous—Robert missed his drive and sent his ball right into the woods.

Strangely enough, instead of apologizing for offering what turned out to be bad advice, the millionaire smiled ironically, as if pleased with the result. Robert was puzzled but decided to say nothing to his host, who had been so gracious up until then.

The millionaire made his shot, and the two men, followed by Hal the caddy, marched off toward the group of trees where Robert's ball had disappeared. As they reached the woods, a telephone rang. It was the millionaire's cellular. Hal hurriedly pulled it out of the old man's bag and handed it over.

"Yes, hello, Mr. President. No, no problem, I'm just playing a few holes with a friend. Yes, hold on a minute, would you?"

Covering the mouthpiece he turned to Robert. "It's the President . . ."

"Oh," Robert said. Although the millionaire had not specified which president, he somehow knew it was THE President, a suspicion that was confirmed when Hal confided, "He's been calling almost every day now that the election campaign's started."

"Is that so?" Robert stammered, trying to sound nonchalant, at the same time wondering why a man who was obviously a multimillionaire, maybe even a billionaire, who lived in a castle on a huge piece of property in the Hamptons, had his own private golf course, and spoke to the President of the United States on a regular basis, would take any interest in a nobody like him, a golf pro who could hardly earn a living and was an abject failure, at least in his own eyes. For an instant he wondered if he wasn't dreaming and almost expected to wake up in some shabby hotel room. Or maybe his accident, coupled with the separation from Clara, had driven him out of his mind. Maybe he was crazy, deluded, one of those psychiatric cases who think they're Napoleon or Julius Caesar or—why not?—the President? After all, hadn't he often dreamed of meeting someone like the old millionaire—a mentor, a guardian angel who would take him under his wing and help make his dreams come true?

As a way of reassuring himself that he wasn't dreaming, he slid his hand into his pocket and felt the thousand-dollar bills he'd won on the practice green. Yes, there they were, crisp and very real. So he wasn't dreaming after all, unless they, too, were part of his fantasy. He pulled one of the bills out of his pocket and looked at it. It seemed quite real, unless his imagination had an amazing capacity for detail . . .

He walked off into the woods to find his ball. The ground between the trees had been cleared of branches. Rays of sun penetrated the treetops, creating an ephemeral atmosphere. Nevertheless, finding his ball among the leaves, pebbles, and pine needles proved difficult.

He walked deeper into the woods. The ball had probably hit a tree and bounced off in God knows which direction. And since Lady Luck had never been his golfing companion— at least that's the way he saw it—he was sure the ball had taken the worst possible bounce and lay buried somewhere where he'd never find it.

He'd been searching for a couple of minutes when he saw a small red fox crouching next to a tree trunk. He had the strangest feeling that the animal was waiting for him. Then he saw his ball between the fox's forepaws. He took a careful step forward, not wanting to alarm the animal, but as he did so, the fox picked the ball up in his mouth and trotted deeper into the forest.

Robert heard a voice behind him calling, "Come on, Freddy, give the ball back to our friend!"

Robert turned and saw the millionaire. The little fox trotted up to Robert and dropped the ball, then walked over to the millionaire, who bent down and scratched the animal between the ears.

"Good boy, Fred," millionaire cooed. "That's a good boy."

Robert picked up the ball and checked the mark to make sure it was his.

"Yeah, Fred," he said, wondering what could possibly happen next, "thanks for the ball!"

7

In Which the Golfer Learns the Secret of Imitation

AS HE HURRIED out of the woods after hitting his ball, still marveling at how smart the little fox had been, Robert inadvertently stepped into a deep puddle, covering his right foot with mud.

"Damn!" he muttered, "these aren't even my shoes."

He limped out onto the fairway and felt acutely embarrassed when the millionaire noticed the mud-covered shoe before he had a chance to clean it off.

"I, uh . . . I guess I didn't see the mud for the trees!" Robert quipped.

"Don't worry about it," the millionaire said. He made a sign to Hal the caddie, who found a shoe kit in one of the golf bags and handed it to his boss.

"Come on, I'll take care of it," the older man said.

Robert walked over without realizing what he meant, and was taken completely by surprise when the millionaire kneeled down in front of him and began undoing the laces of his right shoe.

"What are you doing?" Robert cried, aghast at seeing someone the millionaire's age kneeling in front of him like a valet.

"What am I doing? I'm taking off your shoe, that's what I'm doing. Lift your foot a moment, would you? If you don't help me, I can't help you."

Robert did as he was told. The old man removed the shoe and placed it on the grass. Then he opened the kit and pulled out a couple of rags, a shoe brush, and some polish. As he set to work he explained, "We have to feel humble toward everyone we meet. Every being is unique, like a shining cup containing the wisdom of his or her own experience. If I place myself above the people I meet, they won't be able to pour their wisdom into my cup. But if I place myself lower than them, their wisdom flows naturally into me, drawn by a kind of spiritual gravity. The technique is sometimes called 'tuning in' to others, and it's an attitude that is much more important than most people realize. That's because no one crosses our path by accident. Each person, even the lowliest hobo or the most difficult or evil character, has something to teach us. They all help us forge our character and develop our ability to love others. In this sense, every person is a potential spiritual master. As long as we find ourselves in conflict with someone, as long as we are not in harmony with that person, he or she still has something to teach us. There's still something about our character that needs to be improved. Whenever you find yourself in conflict or suffer a setback, whether it happens at work or in your personal life, ask yourself the following questions: What can this situation or this person teach me? Why did I meet this person at this particular moment in my life?

"When you find the answer, you'll have learned a new lesson and taken another step on the road to wisdom. At the same time, the conflict or problem you're experiencing will disappear automatically. So many people ignore this rule, simple as it may be. We don't appreciate others because we lack humility. We are blind as we walk through life. We hold a mirror up in front of us, seeing only ourselves, unable to see anyone else. That's why most people always think they're right and others are wrong. They never really communicate with other people, they just tell them what they think. Everyone ends up isolated, cut off in their own little mental cocoon. That's why wars have been going on for centuries, because no one tries to see the other person's point of view before passing judgment."

He paused, and his expression, which had grown somber, seemed to regain its usual lightness.

"Now," he said, "let's get back to the business of your shoe."

He picked up the shoe and began wiping the mud off with a rag. After a few seconds, he glanced up and said, "Relax! Sit down and take a load off!"

Robert did as he was told. When the millionaire opened the can of polish, Robert reached for a rag and said, "At least let me do that."

"No, no," the millionaire insisted. "I'm the most qualified person around here to shine your shoe. If you're wondering why, it's because I must have shined ten thousand pairs of shoes in my life."

"Ten thousand pairs?"

"That's right. I entered the job market at the tender age of fourteen, as a shoeshine boy. My father died when I was young, and I had to support myself."

"I'm sorry, I—"

"Don't be. Remember I said there's always time to be un-happy tomorrow or the next day? Well, the same goes for being sad or sorry. Save your sadness and tears for when they're really needed. It's kind of strange, don't you think? No one knows what death is all about, yet everyone gets sad when someone they know dies. I think it's pure egoism. Who knows, maybe all those dead people are watching *us* from the great beyond, sad because we're still alive, hoping we'll join them soon."

"I don't know, I haven't given it much thought."

"That's normal. Most people don't. You let other people do your thinking for you."

He rubbed more polish on Robert's shoe.

"Life is strange, I have to admit. You know, I really started making my fortune shining shoes."

"A fortune, at two bucks a pair?"

"That's right. It often happens that way. Things we con-sider trivial or useless lead to bigger things. It's the same with clients who hardly bring in any profit, but who intro-duce us to bigger clients or help us understand things that come in handy once we get involved in more important deals. It wasn't the two dollars a pair that made me rich. It was my spot on Wall Street. All kinds of very wealthy, very powerful men became my customers. And while I was shining their shoes, I did exactly what I just explained to you—I let them fill me up with their wisdom and experi-ence. I asked questions and listened to what they had to say. I observed them—the way they dressed, the way they walked, the way they talked. I tried to understand their secret, how they managed to acquire so much charisma and authority. I listened to the way they spoke to each other and asked myself what made them different from other people, why they had distinguished themselves, pulled away from the pack so to speak, and made a fortune. I gradually became convinced that I, too, could one day become a part of that elite group, the happy few, and pay someone to shine my shoes.

"I also realized that getting there wouldn't be so difficult after all, that these men whom I got to see up close were not really more intelligent than others who were less successful. What made them different was their confidence, their determination. They saw themselves differently from the way most people do. They had developed a totally positive self-image, and a part of that image required getting their shoes shined by someone else. In fact, some of them regarded themselves a little too highly. I remember a game I used to play. It tested my ability to judge people and showed me which of my customers were excessively proud. Also made me a few extra bucks."

"What was that?"

"Well, when a customer paid me with a five-dollar bill, I'd open my eyes wide and pretend I was overwhelmed by his generosity, assuming of course that I was supposed to keep the change. Four times out of five they were too proud to ask for their money back!"

Robert laughed. "I have to admit I did the same thing a couple times teaching golf."

"I can laugh about it now, but it was tough at the time. I was an orphan, trying to make an honest living for myself. We all have to start somewhere. In any case, that's how I got my first real job. I made the mistake of trying the trick on the same person twice. He was a rich businessman, and fortunately for me he had a good sense of humor. He gave me his card and told me to call him when I was eighteen. Said he'd have a job for me. So that's what I did, and he kept his word. You see, all roads lead to Rome, but you have to be resolute and take the first step."

"Or even better, hop on a passing train," Robert joked.

The millionaire paused and gazed into the distance, perhaps seeing himself as a young man, just starting out. After a moment he said, "I did learn one important truth being a shoeshine boy, though."

"What's that?"

"All wealthy people wear very expensive shoes. No doubt that's why they say you can judge a man's worth by his shoes . . ."

Robert burst out laughing. "If my worth as a golfer is to be judged by my muddy shoe . . ."

"I'm working on it, I'm working on it, don't worry."

It was true that the millionaire worked with extraordinary enthusiasm. Robert marveled at how concentrated the old man seemed to be. After removing every spot of mud, he spread the wax so zealously he actually looked like he was enjoying himself. When the wax was dry, he began shining the shoe with a brush, talking as he worked.

"What I was doing by observing those people was actually a kind of imitation, although I didn't realize it at the time. They say we become who we imitate, and that's what happened to me. One of the beauties of spiritual laws is that they seem to function without our understanding them or even knowing about them. All you have to do is apply them with constancy and love, which is what you should be doing when you play golf. These laws can be applied to all aspects of life. Imitating great people who came before us is like climbing on the shoulders of a giant. When you reach that height, you automatically see farther than others and save all the time it took for your predecessor to learn the things he did. In other words, you don't have to reinvent the wheel. You should do what I did when I was a shoeshine boy for rich stockbrokers. Watch the greats of golf on video, go to tournaments and see how the best in the world play. Let their skill and energy impregnate you, until you literally become one of them.

"Of course, you also have to develop your own personal style. You are unique, just as every beautiful golf shot is unique. Remember, no two fingerprints are alike, even though there are billions of people on this earth. By studying great players, you absorb their qualities, their determination, and their courage, without even knowing it. If you do that, you will become great yourself one day. Imitate them, and at the same time be yourself . . . It takes intelligence to do that. But first make them an object of meditation. Contemplate them, imagine you *are* them. Contemplation is the noblest form of imitation. Never forget that many great men were once excellent imitators."

He fell silent and continued polishing Robert's shoe. He applied himself with such enthusiasm—one could even say love—that his face seemed to shine with an inner light. He looked like a child, aware of nothing else but the task at hand. Sometimes a sound escaped his lips. It sounded like "hum" or "om," as if he was chanting some sacred syllable.

Robert was intrigued. He looked on without saying anything, then glanced over at Hal the caddie as if seeking advice on how to behave in such a situation. Hal seemed to understand his silent question, smiled amiably, and shrugged as if to say, "There's nothing you can do about it, so you might as well enjoy it."

The millionaire stopped brushing and regarded the shoe for a moment. Apparently dissatisfied, he set to work again. It was then that Robert had a strange experience. Looking at the millionaire, he suddenly felt something race through his entire being, like a jolt of energy. He thought about how tense he'd been these last few days—more than that, these last few months, years even. He recalled how impatient he'd become the previous evening just because his old Riviera wouldn't start. As if that was serious, as if his petty little problems were so important they could ruin his whole existence. In short, as if life owed him something.

It suddenly occurred to him that the millionaire, this old man working so diligently at polishing his shoe, was in fact a lot younger, a lot less bitter and impatient than he was. The thought brought tears to his eyes. They welled up so quickly he had to turn his head in shame and wipe them away.

The millionaire laid the brush down, held up Robert's gleaming shoe, and admired his handiwork with obvious satisfaction, happy as an artist before his latest masterpiece or a businessman looking at last year's profit sheet.

"There you go," he said, "good as new."

"Thanks."

"My pleasure. Next time I'll charge by the hour."

Robert chuckled, although he was still overwhelmed by his thoughts of a moment before. He slipped the shoe on and got ready to play his next shot. Before he could do so, however, the millionaire asked him another question.

8

In Which the Golfer Discovers His Inner Power

"WHAT WAS THE last thing that went through your mind before hitting that tee shot into the trees?"

"My last thought . . . hold on a minute . . . I think it was: Don't hit the ball into the trees."

"That was a mistake."

"A mistake?"

"Yes. You slipped into one of the most common dark states of the golfer: Fear."

"Fear?"

"Correct. In addition to being angry over your double bogey on the previous hole, which is another dark state, you let yourself become afraid of driving the ball into the trees."

Robert had a different view. "I'd say I just pushed my tee shot, a mistake I sometimes make under pressure."

"Yes. But what I want you to find out is why you pushed it. And I think the reason is because you don't know the subtle power of fear."

Robert was really curious now, so he listened carefully to what the old man had to say about fear.

"A philosopher once said, 'What I fear most will come to pass.' The fear you felt on the tee was only based on a thought. But it was that thought that dominated your mind. All your thoughts tend to become concrete, even more so during a round of golf. The great psychologist Carl Jung once said, 'All that stirs in the subconscious desires to become real.' Golfers are especially susceptible to this law. If, in your subconscious mind, you think you don't deserve to win a tournament, then you will lose. If you're trying to avoid a water trap or playing a hole that always gives you trouble, even though you don't know why—some golfers call them nightmare holes—then telling yourself, Don't hit the ball into the water! or Don't double bogey like you did last week! will only multiply your chances of making the mistake, instead of protect you. How many times have you heard someone say, 'I knew it! I always do that!' after making the same mistake twice?"

"So what should I do?"

"In each golfer there are actually two persons. The exterior golfer, the one we see, who has a great swing, practices three hours a day or plays once a week, is of such and such a height and weight. And then there's the inner golfer, whom no one else can see, but who sometimes has amazing power. Your inner golfer remembers every golfing event of your life, your great shots, your nightmare holes, your victories and defeats. It's the inner golfer who makes the difference between someone who loses and someone who wins. If the inner golfer thinks in the right way, the exterior golfer plays better no matter what his physical qualities may be. If, however, the exterior golfer cannot communicate properly with the inner golfer, then the inner golfer will not be thinking right, and there is really no hope of success, no matter how many hours you spend on the driving range or how many rounds you play. And this is even more true under pressure, because the more pressure there is, the more you have to rely on your inner golfer. It is the inner golfer who takes over under extreme pressure, so that instead of bogeying a hole you can come back and make an amazing shot out of the sand trap that not only saves the par but puts your ball in the cup for a birdie. It's your inner golfer who hits that unbelievable three-wood to within five feet of the flag. But it's also the inner golfer who misses that crucial three-foot putt, hooks a drive into the trees, or sends an easy approach shot into the lake, the same shot you hit perfectly hundreds of times in practice."

"How is that possible? How can your inner golfer play so brilliantly one day and so abysmally the next?" asked Robert.

"Well, try to think of your inner golfer as a tourist, arriving in a country for the first time, unable to speak the language. He has no grammar, no syntax, and his vocabulary is limited to a few words he memorized on the airplane."

"My inner golfer is a tourist . . . I'm not sure I understand."

"Wait, I'll explain. Imagine that this tourist is walking down a deserted street in a city he doesn't know. He hears someone shouting. He turns around and sees a man of doubtful appearance gesticulating at him. He hurries on his way, only to glance back and see the man chasing him. He starts running, takes the next turn to try and escape, and finds himself in an alley with no way out. The stranger enters the alley and tries to talk to the tourist in his own language. What he says is: 'I'm not a thief, I don't want to hurt you.'

"Now, say you're the tourist. What words do you think you would stand out in your mind from that message?"

"The words *thief* and *hurt*, I guess," Robert said.

"Exactly!" The millionaire was pleased that Robert seemed to understand. "Now the stranger holds up an object and says, 'Your wallet . . .' What do you think the tourist takes that to mean?"

"That the stranger is a thief and wants my wallet. If I don't hand it over, I'll get hurt, maybe even killed."

"Right again. But then the tourist searches his pockets for his wallet and realizes it isn't there. He looks up in a panic and recognizes his wallet in the stranger's hand. The stranger smiles and hands it over. End of story."

"It's a little how I felt when I ran into your fox in the woods. I thought he was going to steal my ball."

"Yes, good fortune often comes in strange disguises. As I so often say, you might as well wait till tomorrow to be un-happy, because it usually takes a little time to see through the disguise. But once you do see, you're even happier, because you didn't let yourself be fooled by appearances.

"Anyway, let's get back to this inner golfer, the tourist. On the last tee the last thing you said to yourself was: Don't hit the ball into the trees. Like the tourist who did not grasp the negation in the sentence 'I am not a thief,' your subcon-scious tuned in to the word *trees*, which became dominant in your mind and made you hit the shot you did, to your great dissatisfaction."

"Well, how could I have avoided it?"

"Simply by giving your subconscious mind the right orders. I'm not saying you should ignore the obstacles on a fairway. On the contrary, you have to be very aware of them, evaluate them fully, and avoid taking any unnecessary

risks. If you have to get past a trap to reach a steeply in-
clined green, then you should probably aim for the center
of the green instead of the flag. That's the way to deal with
real hazards. The next step, however, requires not thinking
about the trap at all. You know it's there, now get the damn
thing out of your mind! And before making the shot, the
one thing you absolutely should *not* say is 'Don't hit the ball
into the sand!'

"Your fear, your hesitation, will almost inevitably prove
disastrous. In the same way, when you can't decide which
club to use, say a five- or a six-iron, make sure that all your
doubts are dispelled before you hit the ball. If not you will
be sending a contradictory message to your inner golfer
and unconsciously letting another dark state of the golfer—
indecision—cloud your mind. 'When in doubt, do nothing,'
the proverb says, and it's a good one, especially when
applied to golf. Eliminate the dark states by waiting until
you know you've made the right choice. Only then can the
brilliant states shine through. Personally, I rely on a rule I
call the hundred percent decision."

"What's that?"

"Well, it's something I discovered while observing myself, an activity people should do more often instead of
staring at the tube. By looking back on my previous business
dealings, I realized that whenever I was one hundred percent
sure about something I succeeded, but whenever I was less
than a hundred percent sure I failed."

"You mean you've experienced failure, too?" Robert
said, genuinely surprised. He had assumed the old man led
a charmed life, that he was immune to failure.

"Certainly. Failure is a natural part of life. Show me a
person who hasn't failed at least once and I'll show you

someone who has never dared to succeed. All great person-alities, whether they're artists, scientists, politicians, or busi-nesspeople like myself, have failed, some more than once. But every time they fall they get up and try again, driven by their inner faith. Problem is, we hear about them only after they attain success. Of course I failed. If I hadn't, I wouldn't have learned anything on this earth, and if I had nothing to learn, I wouldn't be here. Simple as that."

He paused, giving Robert a moment to digest what he'd said, then continued.

"But back to the question of indecision . . . When you hesitate between two clubs or two ways of playing a shot, especially if it's a difficult shot or one that is going to get you out of trouble, take all the time you need. It takes more time to repair the damage caused by a bad decision than to make the right choice. A couple of minutes more never killed anyone. But once you make a decision, don't question it. Put all your doubts aside, address the ball in complete confidence, and make your shot.

"When you allow yourself to be influenced by fear or doubt you are letting in a dark state and ignoring a brilliant state. You have to nourish the light burning within you and let it shine for all to see. Actually it's a very easy thing to do, except that ninety-nine percent of the time people forget, which is why ninety-nine percent of the people who play golf aren't great golfers."

9

In Which the Golfer Learns to Visualize His Shots

THE GOLFER LOOKED at the old man and thought: Nobody ever talked to me like that. With such care. With such love. As if he was my father. As if I was his son . . .

The millionaire said, "Let me explain another great spiritual law, one that applies to golf as much as to anything else."

"I'm all ears," Robert said, curious to know more.

"Every thought, every image that runs through your mind, has a concrete, very real existence. In addition, thoughts and images tend to translate into events in the real world. That's why all great golfers, who by the way are also great thinkers and not just hitting machines as many people assume, visualize their shots before playing them. One of the greatest golfers of all time, Jack Nicklaus, had this to say: 'The first thing I do is *see* the ball where I want it to be, nice and white, sitting on the lovely green grass. Then I change scenes and see the ball flying through the air, heading toward the exact spot I want it to go. I can see its trajectory, its height, I see it hooking or fading, and finally bouncing along the grass until it stops. Then there's a kind of fade out, and in the next scene I see myself making the swing that is going to turn that shot into a reality.'

"Fred Couples does more or less the same thing. Just before hitting the ball, he visualizes the best shot he ever made with that particular club and tries to repeat it. That's the way he communicates with his inner golfer, by using a visual command. He doesn't say, I mustn't overshoot the green, I mustn't hit the ball into the trap . . . He simply excludes those images, eliminating the possibility of a mistake by visualizing the shot he wants to play and leaving no room for any misunderstandings or contradictions, which so often happen when you think in negatives. All he sees is the ideal result.

"Jesus, the greatest psychologist of all time—and who would have made an excellent golfer, by the way—asked his disciples to do the same thing when he said: 'When you pray, pray as if you have already received what you are asking for, as if all your wishes have been granted.' He did not say, 'Think about all the obstacles that can prevent your dreams from coming true. Analyze them, weigh them carefully, and beware of them.'

"I've often heard that great players are completely confident they'll sink a putt, even if they're in the three-putt zone. And, in fact, it is more important to be sure of yourself than to be able to evaluate the curve of the green or the distance of the shot with absolute accuracy. Because if you aren't completely confident, if you can't visualize that ball falling into the hole before you hit it, then you'll miss more putts than you sink, even the easy ones of three or four feet. Great golfers cultivate confidence and let the brilliant states of the golfer shine through. They see the ball dropping into the cup even from thirty feet away. They are driven by the single-minded conviction, a conviction some people might consider absurd, and which is in fact a kind of magic, that they can sink any putt, no matter how long, even if the statistics say they have only one chance in a hundred. They place their confidence in life and in the infinite power of their inner guide."

"Sounds a little too simple to me."

"Well, who ever said success was complicated?"

"Sorry, I should have kept my big mouth shut!"

"Not at all. You think like most other people, as I've noticed on a number of occasions since we met. In other words, you tend to repeat things that others have told you. Your ideas aren't your own, they're clichés, believed by the vast majority of people. Unfortunately, the vast majority do not succeed in life. You should therefore be wary of what most people think."

"You're right. From now on I'll try to be more original."

"Originality is one of the greatest gifts you can offer yourself."

After a pause the millionaire continued, "Great golfers make a vision of the ideal shot their dominant thought; they fill their entire mind with it, leaving their inner golfer no choice but to succeed, protecting themselves against contradictory messages and all other forms of dark states, which can do nothing but harm. I've always made use of these spiritual laws in my business dealings. Before undertaking an important project that seems unrealistic or downright insane to other more 'reasonable' people, I already *see* it succeeding. Of course I also do market studies, figure out costs, evaluate risks, and so on. But I would say that the most important thing is to visualize the project as a success. Good judgment, prudence, and, above all, absolute confidence in the infallibility of these spiritual laws, along with clear images of success—positive events, fortuitous meetings, and so on—enabled me to accomplish all that I have."

"I think I've got a long way to go," Robert said humbly. "I've failed so many times, for so many years, that I guess I don't have much confidence left in myself."

The old man was touched by Robert's sincerity. "You may have a lot of work to do, but, as a Chinese proverb says, even a journey of a thousand miles starts with a single step. Well, why not start your journey now? On your next shot, visualize yourself hitting the ball exactly as you want to. Impregnate your mind with that image. Let it explode in your head like a bright light, clearing away all the darkness. And tonight when you go to bed, talk to your inner golfer. Help him make you the person you really and sincerely want to be. Repeat this formula out loud a hundred times before you fall asleep: 'Every day, in every way, I am getting better and better, and I am becoming a great golfer.' Can you say that?"

Robert found the words awkward. "Every day . . . in every way, I am getting better and better and . . . and . . . I am becoming a great golfer."

"Good. Try it for a few days. If you can maintain your faith in the power of these spiritual laws, you may be surprised. Because, Robert, you are on the threshold of a great transformation, one that will astonish your friends and even yourself. The bitter past is soon to be replaced by a sweeter present. You will be constant in your brilliance. Every shot you make will bring you closer to perfection, closer to that state of mind that only great champions attain. I know there's a champion slumbering inside you. All you have to do is awaken him and you will accomplish marvelous things. You've already had a taste of how it feels. You know what it's like to hit four birdies in a row. You almost feel like you're somebody else, as if you're outside your own body, observing. But it *is* you, a fully realized you. It's like flying above the clouds in a small plane, only now you have a permanent ticket! You don't have to come back to earth, ever. All you have to do is let the brilliant states shine through. They're always there, waiting to clear away the darkness. That is your natural state. Not the low-level flying you've been doing for the last few years!"

Robert was deeply affected by the millionaire's speech. No one had ever spoken to him like that, with so much care and conviction. Neither had anyone ever said things as original—or as strange.

"When you attain this remarkable state," the millionaire went on, "not only will your golf game be completely transformed, you won't be the same person anymore. You will be the man you were destined to be. Your life will be filled with light and joy. What I've described is only a taste of what's to come, a taste of the nectar of the gods. You'll understand that prowess on the golf course is only a stepping-stone, a way of disciplining the mind and ultimately overcoming your limited self to find out who you really are. It will be like throwing away your crutches, freeing yourself of old habits and false images, and finally confronting your true nature. You'll understand that no matter what other people say—your peers, your supposed friends, your parents—you possess what it takes to be a great champion. Starting today, every shot, every game, every tournament will represent one more step toward the realization of your dreams. You'll shine, light will radiate around you like a halo as your brilliance on the golf course gets brighter and brighter. Everywhere you turn, you'll find only the fruits of victory. And one day, if you persevere, you'll attain the highest and most brilliant state any golfer can hope to achieve."

"What state is that?" Robert asked.

10

In Which the Golfer Discovers the Real Love of Golf

"SIMPLY PUT, IT'S a state of love—love for the game. When you learn to love each and every situation you find yourself in, even those that are extremely difficult and which caused you to react with anger, hate, or frustration in the past, and when you've achieved the state of detachment that characterizes all great golfers, you will feel a wave of love flowing out of you at every moment. You will experience each lie of the ball, each hole you play, each round, each tournament as an adventure, an opportunity to perfect your own awareness of the game.

"Golf is one sport that can never be completely mastered, no matter how close a person gets. Maybe that's why so many people find it fascinating. But it is a game that you can learn to love to perfection. To do that you have to let the brilliant states of the golfer, which are just another form of love, shine through. Let them penetrate all aspects of your life, all the people you come in contact with. As you do, you'll acquire the profound certitude that every situation, no matter how difficult or unpleasant, is perfect, and thus transform your vision of the game of golf and your life."

"I can't help thinking all this sounds too easy to be true."

"Take it from me, love is the greatest challenge—and the greatest achievement. More than ambition, more than perseverance, more than determination, more than the ability to visualize, more than courage, more than practice, it is the love of the game that enables some to achieve greatness. There are lots of brilliant states of the golfer, but love is the highest, encompassing all others. Love is the culmination of light. Saint Paul didn't play golf, but what he said sums up what it means to be a great golfer, at least in my opinion. His words have guided me throughout my business career and comforted me in my moments of despair."

The millionaire paused briefly. His face became transfigured as he gazed off into the distance and quoted Saint Paul from memory: "'Yea, though I speak the tongues of men and angels, I am but a clanging cymbal without love. Yea, though I possess the power of prophecy and all knowledge, though I understand the mysteries and move mountains with my faith, I am nothing without love. Love is patient and caring, not proud or jealous. Neither is love arrogant or brutal. Love takes no pleasure in the misfortune of others, rejoices only in their fulfillment. Love accomplishes all, trusts in all, hopes in all, bears all. Love is never-ending.'"

He fell silent. Robert, overwhelmed by emotion, felt moved to the very depths of his heart in a way he could not explain. It was a feeling he had never experienced before, and his eyes filled with tears.

The millionaire seemed to come back from a faraway place. "If you don't love the game, you might as well give up your ambitions right now. Forget about becoming a champion."

"But I do love golf," Robert cried.

"Really? If you love the game so much, why did you get so angry on the last hole?"

For the first time Robert detected a hint of impatience in the millionaire's voice. He knew he was right. In fact, he was amazed at how much the old man had taught him after watching him play for only a few minutes. Incredible as it seemed, they had not even finished the second hole! Before he could come up with a response, the millionaire gently chastised him.

"Who do you think you are, anyway? Are you trying to tell me you're never supposed to miss a shot? Even the greatest golfers screw up occasionally. What gives you the right to become angry? Have you ever considered that there are people out there who would give everything they own to possess a body and mind like yours, to be healthy enough to play this wonderful game, to walk out in the fresh air on a gorgeous summer morning, down those spectacular fairways, among those magnificent trees? Are you so jaded, so bitter that you moan and groan at the slightest setback? Are you so spoiled and blind that you can't see what a wonderful opportunity it is just to be alive? If you really love the game of golf, then don't waste your time and energy on futile emotions. When you feel anger rising inside you, remember the words of Saint Paul: 'Without love, I am nothing.' Without love, a golfer is nothing and will never achieve greatness. Love gives you the patience and will to succeed. Love is not arrogant or violent, angry or vindictive. Love overcomes all obstacles. That's the real secret of becoming great."

"Do you really believe I can become a great golfer one day?"

"Well, don't you think you'd better ask *yourself* that question?"

11

In Which the Golfer Decides to Risk Everything

WHEN THEY FINISHED the round, the millionaire invited Robert to join him on his terrace for lunch, during which they continued their conversation.

"You didn't answer when I said you should ask yourself whether or not you believe you can become a great golfer."

Robert frowned. He had hoped the millionaire had forgotten about that. But it seemed the old man never forgot anything and always asked the most difficult questions—probably because they had to be asked.

"Well, I have a steady job teaching, as I said. So it doesn't really matter what I believe or not, does it?"

"Obviously, if you avoid the issue."

"And you think I'm avoiding the issue?"

"If you haven't got the courage to quit your job, then you probably don't believe in yourself. And if you don't leave the job, you'll never become a champion, you'll never find out if you have what it takes or not. It comes down to a question of faith, as you see. That's why I think it's important that you ask yourself the question—do you believe you have what it takes?"

"If I didn't have to support myself, I think I'd give it another shot."

The millionaire reached into his jacket pocket, extracted a checkbook and pen, and said, "You won ten thousand dollars this morning . . ."

"Eleven thousand," Robert corrected him.

"Eleven thousand, of course," the millionaire said. "How much do you think it would take to keep you in golf balls while you tried to qualify for the P.G.A. tour one more time?"

As he said this, he opened the checkbook, wrote the date and Robert's name, then looked up, waiting for an answer.

"I don't know . . ."

"You're afraid, aren't you? I hope you're not one of those people who keep saying, 'If only . . .' If only they'd had the chance, they would've started their own business, or if only they'd met the right person, they would've married, had children, and made a life for themselves. But then when the chance comes along, they're too afraid to take it, afraid to fail. People like that are liars—they lie to others, and, even worse, they lie to themselves."

"No, it has nothing to do with fear."

"What is it then?"

"Well, the money . . ."

"I'm offering to solve that problem for you," the millionaire said. "I'm ready to write you a check for whatever amount you think you need. All I want to know is how much. Frankly, I think you have a serious problem as far as money is concerned. Maybe that's why you never won big. Well, I'm waiting . . ."

"I can't just take your money."

"Alright, I won't give it to you. I'll lend it to you, interest free, for three months. Does that make you feel better? Three months from now, when you've qualified for the tour and get a chance to win the U.S. Open, you can start paying me back."

"And what if I don't qualify?"

"Listen, if you keep looking for reasons to fail, to not take the plunge, then I can only conclude I've made a mistake about you and that I shouldn't lend you the money."

"Okay," Robert said, almost in a panic at seeing this golden opportunity slip away, "I'll do it. Lend me as much as you want. I'll work things out somehow."

"Good! Finally a positive word!" the millionaire exclaimed, smiling broadly. He glanced at Robert, thought for a moment, then said, "How about twenty-five thousand? Will that be enough? That'll give you thirty-six thousand in all. It's not a fortune, but you should be able to last three months."

The offer was way beyond Robert's wildest expectations. He tried to sound nonchalant as he replied, "Oh, yeah, I think I can make do on that."

"Do you need more?"

"No, no, twenty-five thousand is fine. Just fine."

"Alright," the millionaire said, entering the amount, signing with a flourish, and handing the check over. "It's a deal."

While Robert contemplated the check with a mixture of disbelief and elation, the millionaire reached for a little bell and rang it.

"Do you want me to . . . to sign some kind of paper?" Robert asked.

"Why?"

"I don't know, so you'll have an IOU or something."

"I can see you don't place much faith in trust. I have your word, don't I?"

"Yes, of course."

"That's good enough for me. I don't need a piece of paper to trust someone. If I can't judge whether a person is honest or not at my age, then I deserve to be taken for a ride. Actually, no one is ever really tricked into doing anything. When your heart is pure, even dishonest people have no choice but to be honest with you, both in affairs of money and in affairs of the heart. Fate decides if somebody is going to steal from you or not. It's all recorded in the big book."

"I don't know how to thank you for this. I hope you never regret placing your trust in me."

"Stop being so pessimistic!" the millionaire said with a smile.

"Sorry."

"You really have a problem with self-confidence, don't you?"

"Well, maybe . . ."

"We don't have a lot of time to work on it, but I think there's a shortcut we can take," said the millionaire with an enigmatic smile. He summoned the butler, who showed up seconds later.

"Henry," the millionaire said, "since our friend here finds himself without a car for the time being, would you ask Edgar to take him to the garage and let him pick one he can use for the next few weeks?"

"Of course, sir."

"Really," Robert protested, "that isn't necessary."

"It would give me great pleasure if you accepted. I do feel partly responsible for the accident, after all. And believe me when I say it won't put me out in the least."

A few minutes later, when Edgar opened the door to the immense garage, Robert understood what the old man meant. There were about a dozen cars inside, none of them your ordinary vehicle. A couple of Jags, a couple of Rolls-Royces, three or four Mercedes, a Porsche Carrera, a white stretch limo, two BMWs, and finally a red Ferrari that Robert especially admired.

"Which one?" Edgar asked nonchalantly, as if he gave away fabulous cars for a living. Robert was flabbergasted. Any car he wanted? He felt like pinching himself to make sure he wasn't dreaming. "I wouldn't recommend the limo, though," Edgar continued, "it's a bitch to drive."

Robert took a step forward, excited as a kid in a candy store. He'd never seen cars like this up close before. He couldn't help but think that the old man must really be loaded to own them all! He stopped beside the Ferrari, the car of his dreams, and just stood there in awe, not daring to tell Edgar that it was the one he wanted.

"So, you like that one?" Edgar asked, as if he was talking about a hat.

"Yeah . . . yeah, I sure do," Robert stammered.

Edgar walked over to a little wall-mounted cupboard and opened the door. Inside were rows of keys. He selected one and handed it to Robert.

"Strange you should pick that one," he said. "It's sorta been waiting for someone like you to come along. No one's driven it since the old man bought it."

As he rolled out of the garage, feeling the car's nervous power through the plush leather seat, Robert was amazed at the twist of fate that had brought him here. Only the night before, broke and depressed, he had almost been killed in a car accident. And here he was with thirty-five thousand dollars in his pocket, driving a brand new Ferrari!

Although he had never placed much importance on material possessions, he could not help but feel elated, proud to be driving what many would agree was the classiest car in the world. His horizons had expanded considerably in the last twenty-four hours!

The car performed to perfection, even better than he had imagined. There was only one thing missing: his beloved Rolling Stones tape—a problem he quickly solved by stopping at the first music store he saw and buying a copy of the Stones' greatest hits. It wasn't as good as the made-to-measure mix he had been playing at the time of the accident, but it would do. The tape started with one of his favorites: "Time Is on My Side."

And for the first time in his life, Robert felt that time really was on his side, as if a page had been turned and a new chapter of his life had begun, a chapter full of light and happiness.

There was still one thing he had to take care of: He had to tell Larry, the manager of the country club where he worked, that he wanted a three-month leave of absence. As expected, Larry, a scrawny fellow with a permanent sneer, was not thrilled.

"You what? Get serious, Rob. There's nothing about a leave of absence in your contract. You get to play seven tournaments a year, max. You're asking for three months for God's sake!"

"That's right."

"Why? Planning to try out for the U.S. Open?"

"As a matter of fact, I am."

"Are you out of your mind? You don't even know if you can qualify. And even if you do, your chances of winning are zip."

"Maybe, but I have to give it one more shot."

"You sure you're feeling okay? I mean, you had a pretty serious car accident yesterday, right? Maybe you got hit on the head. Maybe you lost touch with reality. Maybe they gave you too much medication!"

"The doctor says I'm fine. My decision is made. When I get back, I'll be in better shape than ever. And if I manage to place in the top ten, the club's reputation will skyrocket."

"Well, I can't guarantee your job'll be waiting when you get back."

"I have to take that risk."

"Don't say I didn't warn you!"

Robert stopped in at the pro shop to say good-bye to a couple of colleagues, then went to the locker room to get his equipment. Seeing the familiar surroundings, he suddenly felt nervous, realizing that he was about to give up his job, his security. But he couldn't turn back now. He'd made a commitment, given his word. There was no way he was going to let the millionaire down.

On his way out of the clubhouse he ran into his father who was walking toward the lounge where he was working. Although he was in his sixties, Robert's dad still made an imposing figure. His gray hair was thick, and there was hardly a wrinkle on his face. It was obvious where Robert had gotten his athletic build and good looks.

"Larry told me what you're up to," his father snapped before Robert could say anything. "Are you crazy? You want to try out for the U.S. Open?"

"Yeah, Dad, I do."

"You're going to lose the best job you ever had."

A group of members crossed the lobby, and Robert's father had to interrupt his condemnation to offer a forced, ingratiating smile. As soon as they were out of earshot, he turned his attention back to his errant son.

"The U.S. Open! You never won a pro tournament in your life, not even a minor one. Give me a break! Suddenly you want to throw everything away for an idiotic, adolescent fantasy?"

"Listen, Dad, I'm sorry to disappoint you. I hope my leaving doesn't make it difficult for you around here. But my decision is final."

He held out his hand but his father refused to shake it. Robert headed for the door. His father shouted after him as loudly as he dared, "You're going to end up on the street! I'm telling you, Robert, you're making a big mistake! You don't have what it takes. You never did, and you never will!"

Robert, knowing it was pointless to argue, just kept on walking, his face impassive although inside he was churning with anguish. His father had never believed in him, had told him in thousands of small ways that he was destined for failure. Is that how a father should behave toward his only son? Couldn't he at least show a little compassion, a little understanding?

Robert knew he'd have to see this through to the end. It was all or nothing now.

He headed for the Ferrari, which he'd left in a visitor's space, and caught sight of Sylvester, the parking attendant, who greeted him with his perpetual eager smile.

"Got some new wheels?" Sylvester asked, running a finger over the gleaming hood.

"Sort of."

"Suits you, I have to admit."

A club member walking to his car, the owner of the red Porsche who had made Robert feel so inferior the day before, took one look at the Ferrari and gaped, letting his cigar drop out of his mouth. Robert waved and got behind the wheel. The guy stooped to pick up his stogie, wondering how a miserable golf pro had managed to get hold of a car like that. Unfortunately, the cigar had fallen into a puddle left by the previous night's storm and was sodden. Robert cruised past, inadvertently sending a spray of muddy water into the guy's face. He stood up, spluttering and mouthing obscenities. Sylvester had a good laugh behind the club member's back—the guy deserved no sympathy after all the times he'd conveniently "forgotten" to leave a tip.

As the Ferrari hugged the winding road through a pine forest bordering rolling fairways, Robert wondered again if he'd done the right thing or made a terrible mistake. At the intersection that led to the main highway, he stopped and took a last look at the stately gray stone clubhouse, its sloping roof towering above the treetops.

Shrugging off his doubts, he gripped the wheel and pressed down a little too hard on the accelerator. The Ferrari sprang forward, leaving a track of burned rubber on the pavement. The car had phenomenal power as well as great lines. Purring along at the speed limit with the travel-poster countryside rolling by, Robert felt his confidence grow. He'd made a decision and now he'd have to see it through. The club, his job—he had to put all that behind him. He had three months to make something of himself, three long months during which anything could happen. And, if things kept moving as fast as they had since yesterday, *everything* would happen! There was no time to brood over the past—the future lay straight ahead! The moment had come to burn bridges, press on, and hope for the best.

He'd done what he had set out to do—get his clubs, tell Larry he was taking some time off, and say good-bye to the friends he'd made on the job. He'd had yet another edifying conversation with his father and informed him of his intentions. Everything seemed to be taken care of except for one last thing, the most difficult on his list. Clara. He had to see Clara. He thought about her constantly. He owed her an explanation.

He hesitated as long as he could, then stopped at a phone booth and made the call. She sounded distant on the phone, said she wasn't ready to see him yet, she was in a hurry, on her way out. But when she said good-bye, he thought he heard her voice quaver for an instant as she stifled a sob. It was a very thin thread, yet he could not help but hope that all was not lost.

He'd have to give her time, that was all. Isn't that what he'd been asking her to do for him for months, years, even? He owed her at least that much.

12

In Which the Golfer Meets Someone Who Believes in Him

WHILE ROBERT DILIGENTLY began practice early the next morning, the millionaire headed into town to attend to an important duty. One of the charitable foundations he supported granted last wishes to children with terminal diseases, and the millionaire took great pleasure in granting these requests in person. With Edgar the chauffeur close on his heels, the millionaire strode into the children's hospital with a cheerful grin, greeting everyone warmly.

Meanwhile, in a small waiting room upstairs, a doctor was in conference with an ill child's parents.

"He hasn't got much longer," the doctor said somberly.

The father, in his early forties, wore a three-piece suit and a pair of heavy-rimmed glasses that emphasized his slightly authoritarian demeanor. The mother, in her late thirties, seemed rather cold and businesslike. She wore a tight-fitting suit, and her black hair was combed severely back. She was obviously uncomfortable, impatient to get the interview over with.

"How much longer?" the man asked.

"We can never be absolutely sure," the doctor replied, "but I'd give your son two, three, maybe six months at the outside. For the moment his condition is stable, and he seems strong enough. But that's a common phase with this type of cancer. When he starts deteriorating again, things will happen very quickly. I know this isn't pleasant for you, but I've always thought it best to be truthful instead of hiding the facts, especially with the parents. I won't say anything to Paul. As his parents, that's up to you, as I explained earlier."

"Well, it doesn't change anything as far we're concerned," the woman said, her voice hard, devoid of emotion. "My husband and I are separating, and we adopted Paul just two years ago . . . Well, we don't intend to abandon him, but neither my husband nor I can take care of him for the next few months. Both of our jobs involve a lot of travel. We have to put Paul's welfare first, and it's obvious he'd be better off staying here, with all the best facilities available, than with either of us. Plus we're living in different cities now, and we'd have to hire full-time nurses . . . You understand, don't you, doctor?"

The physician said nothing, hoping what he really thought wasn't showing on his face. The woman's husband seemed less sure it was the right thing to do. He shook his head and gritted his teeth, trying to look like someone who had been forced into making an unpleasant decision.

The doctor led them back into the sickroom where little Paul was waiting. He was a handsome, eager boy of ten, with a head of curly blond hair and very dark eyes that were made more expressive by the ravages of disease.

"Your father and I are going to take a vacation, Paul," the woman said.

"When are you coming back?"

"We're not sure exactly, but you mustn't worry. If you're a good boy, we'll bring you a wonderful present. How's that?"

"Really, Mom?"

"Really. But you have to promise to be a good boy."

"I promise."

The mother put on a big show of giving him a hug.

"I love you so much, Mom," the boy sighed. The woman turned away and it was the father's turn. "You too, Dad," Paul said. "Thanks for being my parents."

"We love you, Paul." The father had trouble controlling his voice. "We love you . . ."

With tears in his eyes, the boy watched them leave, not knowing they had no intention of coming back, that it would be the last time he'd see them in his short life.

In the lobby downstairs, the somber group passed by the millionaire, who was chatting with a little girl in a wheelchair. The doctor, who knew him for his good works, stopped to talk while Paul's parents headed for the exit. The doctor told the millionaire about the poor boy, and the millionaire gazed sternly at the retreating couple, sneaking away like two thieves.

A few minutes later the millionaire and Edgar were in Paul's room. The boy was almost hysterical with laughter as Edgar clowned around pretending to be a chimpanzee. Finally the millionaire asked the question, "Tell me, Paul, what is it you wish for most in the world? What would you most like to do?"

"Can it be anything I want?" the boy said, excited.

"Anything! I might not be able to get it for you, but you can always ask."

"Well," the boy said, his eyes shining, "what I'd like to do most is play with the greatest golfer in the world."

"Is that so? Do you play golf, Paul?"

"Sure! I have a twelve handicap, but I've only been at it for two years."

"A twelve handicap, that's excellent. That's better than me, and I've been practicing forever. If you played with the monkey over there, you'd have to give him at least twenty strokes."

Edgar, who did not in the least mind being teased, made a face that set the boy laughing again. The millionaire, meanwhile, thought of a way to kill two birds with one stone. At the same time he marveled at the mysterious—often hidden—perfection of life.

"Well, Paul, how about tomorrow? Feel up to playing a round with him tomorrow?"

Paul looked at Edgar, who was still pulling funny faces, shaking his head so hard he sent his hat flying into the air.

"You mean with him?"

"No, not with him," the millionaire said. "With the greatest golfer in the world! In fact, you've never heard of this man, but take it from me—he's the best, and soon everyone will know his name."

"Cool!" said the boy.

* * *

The millionaire arranged for Paul to spend the night at his Hamptons residence. The next morning, out in the rose garden where Paul had already picked a huge bouquet, he introduced the boy to Robert.

"I picked these for Mom," Paul informed them in all innocence. "She's coming to see me soon."

The millionaire felt a pang of sympathy. "That's very nice, Paul," he said. Robert, who had been told about the boy's predicament—his cancer, the cruel departure of his adoptive parents, and the little white lie concerning his own stature as the greatest golfer in the world—had a hard time holding back his tears. Seeing how trusting the boy was, still believing in his parents' love, his first thought to pick a bouquet of flowers for his mother, was enough to break any man's heart.

"Well, Paul," the millionaire said, "here he is, the greatest golfer in the world, just like I promised."

The boy took a step forward, fumbling with the bouquet. Henry the butler relieved him of the flowers. Beaming with admiration, he finally shook hands with Robert.

"Gee, this is totally awesome. Can we . . . I mean . . . ?" He turned to the millionaire.

"You want to get out there and play a round right away, don't you, son?"

"Yeah, if we can."

"I don't see why not. That's what we're here for, right, Robert?"

"I'm ready if you are."

Fifteen minutes later, the threesome was heading for the first tee. Paul had been equipped with glove, shoes, and a set of juvenile clubs. Robert teed off first. Not wanting to disappoint young Paul—after all, he had been billed as the greatest golfer in the world—he hit a spectacular drive, three hundred yards right down the middle of the fairway.

"Wicked!" cried the boy. "I've never seen anyone hit a ball like that, not even on TV!"

The millionaire hit his standard drive, about two hundred and twenty yards, slightly left of center. Paul was about to tee up when the millionaire's pet fox scampered out from behind a hedge and sat down right in front of the boy.

"Freddy!" the millionaire called. "What're you doing? Let Paul play his shot!"

But Paul seemed to forget about golf for the moment. He dropped his club, bent down, and began petting Freddy's snout. The little red fox seemed to enjoy the attention immensely.

"He's so beautiful!" Paul exclaimed.

"His name's Freddy, and he lives here on the golf course. I get the feeling you two are going to become good friends."

"I know we will," Paul said, more to the fox than to either of the two men.

Watching him, Robert felt a wave of regret—he'd been such an idiot with Clara, avoiding any kind of commitment, afraid to start a family. They could have had a child just like Paul. Instead he was alone, abandoned by the only person who had believed in him all these years. At least now he had the millionaire to believe in him. And Paul, of course, although his confidence was based on a lie. But this bending of the truth gave the boy at least a few moments of happiness; it made his dream come true before he died.

"Okay, Freddy," the millionaire said, "we're playing a game here. Let Paul hit his tee shot, would you?"

The fox seemed to understand and trotted over to the edge of the fairway, where he sat and watched like a spectator. He followed the threesome all around the course. The millionaire said it was the first time he'd ever done that.

The morning unfolded as the millionaire hoped it would. It was a different kind of pressure he had arranged for Robert—not wanting to disappoint the sick boy, he believed that Robert would try his very best. The ploy worked to perfection—Robert came through with flying colors, shooting an incredible 31 for nine holes, five under par.

After the round, the millionaire left Robert and Paul alone, sipping glasses of ice-cold lemonade. Freddy the fox came and sat with them—he didn't seem to want to leave Paul's side.

"I'll never be able to play like you," Paul sighed.

"I think you could. The potential is there. What did you shoot, 44?"

"Yeah. I was aiming for 39. I never shot under 40 before."

"You know, when I was your age, I didn't play as well as you. You could be a champion by the time you're twenty."

"I don't think so. I won't live that long."

It was the last thing Robert had expected to hear. He'd thought the boy didn't know.

"Why do you say that?"

"I overheard the nurses talking; they thought I was asleep, but I wasn't. I know Mom loves me too much to tell me. I've got six months tops."

"Oh," Robert sighed, momentarily at a loss. He sought desperately for the right thing to say. "Listen, you can get better. If you believe in yourself, you can get better. Things have a way of working out . . ."

"My disease is incurable."

"Doctors make mistakes. They're human, like everyone else. A friend of mine was once told he had cancer. He stopped smoking, drove himself crazy. A month later he found out it was all a mistake. The files had gotten mixed up. One good thing though, he didn't start smoking again!"

"No, this isn't a mistake. I know I'm sick, I feel it inside me . . ."

Paul grew pale even as he spoke—playing the nine holes had taken a lot out of him. The day, which had started so well, seemed about to end on a somber note. As they walked side by side toward the house, Robert promised himself he would do everything in his power to make this boy's dream come true. He'd qualify for the P.G.A. tour, he'd sweat blood and tears to do it. And then, God willing, he'd win the U.S. Open.

13

In Which the Golfer Faces His First Test

EARLY THE NEXT morning, instead of heading out to the driving range for a little warm-up as he usually did, Robert climbed into his Ferrari (it had been as easy to start thinking of the car as "his" as it was going to be hard to part with it when the time came!) and drove to Paul's hospital.

He told the nurse on duty that he was there on behalf of the millionaire. Mentioning the old man worked like a magic formula—doors opened and faces lit up. Robert asked to see the boy's medical report.

He read it over twice and finally had to accept the facts: The disease was terminal, nothing could be done. Life expectancy was a few months at most. Robert was about to hand the file back when an idea popped into his head apparently out of nowhere. Maybe it was the pile of unused report sheets on the nurse's desk. Maybe it was an inner voice telling him what to do, something that had been happening more and more often since the millionaire had taught him to observe his own thoughts.

In fact, he had been repeating the mental formula the millionaire had suggested he use every day: "Every day, in every way, I am getting better and better . . ."

His sixth sense was improving. He had an intuition about how to play a ball that he didn't have before. He noticed all kinds of little things about his game that had cost him shots—and sometimes a tournament—in the past. As his confidence grew, he felt a strange transformation taking place inside him.

In any case, there it was—a way to help Paul, just like the millionaire had helped them both by telling the boy that Robert was the greatest golfer in the world, with the result that Paul's dream came true and Robert played better than ever before. The millionaire's private course wasn't the toughest Robert would have to face. Nevertheless, he'd shot five birdies, all because of a little white lie. No one should lie, Robert thought, but at the right time and place, for the right reasons, a lie seemed to work wonders. And when you came right down to it, it wasn't even a lie—just an affirmation of faith, the faith of an innocent child. There was no way Robert could have let Paul down.

Faith and words . . . the millionaire had spoken at length about the power of words. Words that could literally bring someone back to life—or kill them. Words that yesterday had made Robert surpass himself on the golf course, words that in the past had made him fail miserably.

So why not use words to help Paul? Who knows, maybe he would recover. It was worth a try.

"Do you think you could make me a photocopy of this report?" Robert asked the nurse.

"Of course, sir, no problem at all."

While the nurse was making the copy, Robert slipped a couple of blank reports off the top of the pile on her desk, quickly folded them, and slipped them into his vest pocket.

An hour later he'd written a new report and had practiced imitating the attending physician's signature until it was almost perfect. The new report was much more favorable, indicating that under no circumstances should Paul discontinue his treatments, that there was real hope of a recovery, and that the disease was not incurable as previously thought.

When Paul read it, he was dumbfounded.

"I told you," Robert said. "I spoke to your doctor. He checked over his tests and found a mistake in the diagnosis. There was some kind of misunderstanding."

Paul was speechless, but the smile that lit up his face was eloquent enough—Robert could see the glimmer of renewed hope springing to life in the boy's heart.

"My parents are going to be even more excited than I am!" Paul exclaimed. "They won't believe it. I can't wait till they get back from vacation!"

Robert smiled sadly. His little plan might have rekindled Paul's hope, but it wouldn't bring back his parents.

In the days that followed, Paul showed signs of improving. His complexion lost some of its pallor, his cheeks took on a rosy tint, his movements seemed livelier, and his appetite returned with a vengeance. It was a beautiful sight for everyone who knew him.

Paul's doctor was amazed and even gave him permission to accompany Robert to a couple of P.G.A. qualifying tournaments. The boy's faith in his new friend worked wonders. Robert played like the greatest golfer in the world and had no trouble qualifying for the tour, a dream he'd given up on long ago.

The ease with which he made the qualifying round surprised no one more than himself. Of course it had taken concentration and effort. But often, just as he was about to commit a mental error that might have cost him a couple of strokes, as had happened so many times in the past, he remembered the "stop" technique the millionaire had taught him. Taking a couple of seconds to think things over, he would identify the dark state of the golfer that was threatening to spoil his game and replace it with a brilliant state.

The technique had not proved infallible, but it did enable him to make the cut and qualify for the prestigious U.S. Open.

Paul didn't congratulate him, not because he wasn't happy for Robert but because it was simply something he expected from the greatest golfer in the world.

"I'm sure you're going to win the championship," he confided.

"Really? Care to tell me why you're so sure?"

"It's simple. The United States is the greatest country in the world, right?"

"Well, a lot of Americans think so."

"Right. But the world is still bigger than the United States, right?"

"True."

"Well, if you're the greatest golfer in the world, and the world is bigger than the United States, then it'll be easy for you to become the U.S. champion."

There was nothing Robert could say to refute the boy's rock-solid logic, so he just nodded and kept quiet. But there was something that bothered Paul deeply—his parents were taking forever to get back from their vacation, and they hadn't called or written for weeks, not even a postcard explaining why they were staying away so long. Maybe something terrible had happened to them, an accident or a robbery or some strange tropical disease.

Robert wondered if it wouldn't be better to tell him the truth instead of letting him worry. On the other hand, the news might have a negative impact on his fragile state of

health. Robert finally decided to wait. The U.S. Open pre-
liminary rounds were scheduled to begin, and the boy was
soon caught up in the feverish preparations, forgetting
about his parents' neglect, at least for the moment.

Robert found himself completely absorbed in the task at
hand. He was about to experience the most important four
days of his life. Four days that would decide his future, and
maybe, just maybe, gain him entrance to a select club—the
club of champions.

The list of competitors was awesome. Robert would be
facing not only the best golfers in the country but the best
from around the world. Among them were U.S. Open, British
Open, and Masters winners, the legends of golf, who could
put on a burst and walk away with the title at any time.

But on Thursday morning, a few hours before his tee-off
time, Robert forced such thoughts out of his mind. If he wanted
to win, he had to come to terms with the idea of beating his
idols. There was no point in playing if he thought the winner's
trophy was inaccessible before he started. Even the greatest
golfers in the world were men just like him, hoping to win,
coveting the prize they had worked so hard to possess.

He had to ward off the dark states of the golfer, otherwise they would paralyze him, destroy him. An opportunity
like this one would never present itself again.

He ate a hearty breakfast and tried to stay as calm as
possible. The millionaire had explained why it was so
important to eat slowly: Chewing each mouthful thoroughly
helped draw out the food's secret energy, made digestion a
lot easier, and forced you to eat less—three crucial advantages
when dealing with stress.

As he swallowed the last of his cereal, Robert recalled the
millionaire's philosophy of life: Live each day as if it were

your first. Let go of the past. Live in the present. At the same time, the wise old man lived each day as if it was his last. He put his whole heart and soul into everything he did, every gesture, every word.

Robert concentrated on forgetting about what was at stake, absorbing himself instead in the present moment. He had to take the tournament one day at a time. One round at a time. One shot at a time. As if each shot were his first, with no burden of past failures weighing on his mind.

He would play each shot with as much concentration and love as he could generate in himself. The tournament would be his testament, his final word. It was time to get out there and prove his worth, and he was ready.

He looked forward to seeing Paul among the spectators. The boy's doctor had given him permission to attend, saying he seemed strong enough. Robert's caddie, although not the most experienced on the circuit, was perhaps the most colorful in his Payne Stewart knickers and matching cardigan. He was certainly the oldest—the millionaire, of course.

Thursday and Friday went by like a dream. Robert not only made the cut, he led the pack after two rounds with a 68 and a 69, playing great golf on the narrow fairways that made the Open so treacherous.

He simply could not believe it!

"See?" the millionaire said. "I told you winning didn't have to be difficult."

It was like a dream. Robert's dream. The dream of a child.

Robert realized that the change in him was completely mental. He was now experiencing the game on another level. Sure, things were happening out there on the golf course: the competitors, the different holes, the crowd, the scoreboard . . . But his game was essentially happening in his mind, each shot was the result of an inner monologue, or, more precisely, a dialogue between his inner golfer and himself.

Robert soon realized that everything the millionaire had told him was true. To win he had to constantly observe his thoughts and accept only those which nourished his inner golfer, allowing the outer golfer—his physical body—to make the best possible shot under any given set of circumstances.

It was hard work keeping all the dark states of the golfer out for hours and days at a time. In fact, it was the *hardest* part about playing the game.

First evaluating the situation properly, calmly—the lie, the distance, the wind, the bunkers, the water.

Then making the right club selection.

Then once that was done, only one thing was left: Thinking about the perfect shot. Only that and nothing else.

The perfect tee shot. The perfect iron shot. The perfect approach shot. The perfect putt. Shot after shot. Hole after hole.

With no dark states of the golfer. With only brilliant states of the golfer. And nothing else.

No fear. No doubts. No anger because he missed the previous shot. No impatience. No risky shots that were not worth it.

Only the clear image of the ideal shot. And silence. And love. And joy. And respect. For each shot. For the game of golf. For life itself.

The magic of the first two days continued through Saturday. Now there were journalists to add to the pressure. Who was this guy? How could a total unknown play three consecutive rounds under par? Saturday's 70 was a slight slip from the previous days' 68 and 69, but he was still leading the pack. Where the hell had he come from? This was a guy who had never even qualified for the tour before, and now he was heading into the final round of the U.S. Open three strokes up! He was an underdog, sure, but was he a choker or a winner? It made great copy.

Robert found the whole thing astounding. He could still hardly believe that everything the millionaire said was actually happening, that by working on his mind he had turned his entire life around.

Unfortunately, the mind cannot transform all things. An hour after his phenomenal win on Saturday, Robert hurriedly made his excuses to a horde of reporters and rushed to the hospital. Paul had suddenly started feeling very ill and had to be taken away in an ambulance.

Back in the hospital room, Robert made sure the boy was comfortably tucked in and assured him he'd be feeling well enough in the morning to come to the final round. Paul wasn't as optimistic.

"Don't worry, if I can't come I'll watch you win on TV."

"I'll do my best," Robert said, his heart going out to the boy.

"What do you mean?" Paul cried.

"Sorry," Robert quickly apologized. "I'll win—I'll win it for you. How's that?"

"Promise?"

"Promise."

If only it were as easy to keep promises as to make them.

That night, back in his room in the millionaire's mansion, Robert got the jitters. He was so nervous he vomited.

It was the first time he had ever experienced a night before Sunday on the Tour.

He tried to use the secrets the old man had taught him. He kept repeating that he was calm, that everything would turn out fine. It was only a mental game. But what a game!

At one o'clock, he finally fell into a restless sleep. Tossing and turning, he had a very strange dream . . .

14

In Which the Golfer Discovers the Terrible Secret of His Childhood

IN ROBERT'S DREAM, the old man invited him for a ride in his limo with Freddy the fox. The millionaire was wearing his golf clothes, and Robert was a bit surprised when he saw that the old man was already wearing his golf shoes. But, after all, he was a bit eccentric.

"Where to, boss?" asked Edgar.

"I thought you knew," said the millionaire.

"Oh, right, sir . . ."

Edgar stepped on it but the millionaire leaned forward to call, "Not this way, Edgar. Go backward."

Robert was intrigued. Backward? He shrugged his shoulders and started playing with the cute little fox.

A few minutes later, the limousine stopped in front of a house that Robert quickly recognized. It was his parents' house, but Robert didn't know why they were there.

"You have to go now," said the old man. "You have to go."

Robert didn't want to go, but Edgar opened the door, indicating that he should leave. Robert reluctantly stepped out of the limousine. The second his foot touched the sidewalk, he was transformed. He became a child, a six-year-old boy, and an instant later he was in his bedroom with all his old toys.

He heard his mother crying. He rushed to her room and saw her sitting on her bed with her head in her hands.

"What's wrong, Mommy?"

"I've lost the bracelet your father gave me for my birthday."

"Don't cry, Mommy. We'll find it." He helped his mother look for it, but with no success. He was about to give up when he heard a sound. He looked up and saw his friend John grinning at him with devilish eyes through the open window. The two boys strongly resembled each other and often were mistaken for twins.

But John had a dark side. So when he saw him at the window, Robert knew right away that John had stolen the bracelet. The young Robert leapt up and chased after his friend.

"Give me the bracelet!" he shouted.

His friend stopped, held out the bracelet to taunt Robert, and said, "Come and get it!"

Robert tackled John and they wrestled. At one point John slipped and fell, breaking a tooth. Robert took advantage of John's distraction and grabbed his mother's bracelet back.

"You'll pay for that!" John shouted, but Robert ignored his threat.

Clutching the bracelet, Robert ran home triumphantly. On his way up to his mother's room, he ran into his father, who was watching TV, his favorite hobby besides fixing himself a drink—an easy task for him since he was a bartender. His father caught sight of the bracelet and shouted, "I knew it! You took it! You should be ashamed of yourself!"

"But Dad, it wasn't me! It was John!"

"Don't lie to me!" His father heaved himself out of his armchair and slapped Robert hard across the face. The young boy fell, hitting his head on the coffee table. He bled and it hurt. But the gash in his forehead was not what was causing his pain.

"You little thief," said his father, who picked up the bracelet and ignored the fact that his son was bleeding. "You'll never do anything decent in your life!"

Robert sobbed . . .

The next instant he was no longer a six-year-old, nor was he at his parents' house. He was in a huge room with a marble floor, marble walls, and even a marble ceiling. He was standing in front of a mirror, looking at the scar on his forehead. It was red and swollen and looked fresh. Now he understood why he'd forgotten how he got it. It simply hurt too much to remember, and time has a way of suppressing painful memories. But they stay deep in the mind, lying dormant. You don't know they're there . . .

His father had slapped him. His father thought he was a liar and a loser. His father didn't believe him or believe *in* him.

Robert heard somebody behind him, breaking his chain of thought. It was the old man walking toward him, wearing patterned knickers and golf shoes without socks. His shoes made a curious sound on the marble floor as he approached. Seconds later, the millionaire was at his side. The old man noticed Robert's scar right away.

"Oh, that's a bad scar you have. Let's see what we can do."

He removed his golf glove and blew into the palms of his hands, then placed his hands on Robert's forehead. After a few seconds of the old man's gentle touch, the scar disappeared as if by magic!

"Thank you," said Robert, astonished. "Thank you very much!" At that moment he felt a tremendous love for the old man, who was standing beside him smiling as if he performed such miracles every day.

Then the old man touched Robert on the temple and said, "We will also remove the scar you have up here." With that he put his glove back on and walked away.

Robert woke up. It took a moment before he realized that he was lying on the bed in one of the numerous rooms in the millionaire's mansion.

He was sweaty, the bedspread in disarray. He had dreamed the whole thing! He remembered everything—the limousine with the old man and the fox, his parents' house, his mother crying, the fight with John, the mysterious meeting with the millionaire in a marble room, his scar cured by magic.

His scar! He dashed to the bathroom and looked in the mirror. The scar was still there, of course. It was only a dream, even though it felt so real.

His face looked ghostly pale under the bright lights. "I don't look so good," he said to himself. "I hope I look better tomorrow on the first tee."

15

In Which the Golfer Is Put to the Final Test

ROBERT WOKE UP at six o'clock, took a cold shower, and headed downstairs to the dining room where the millionaire was already having coffee.

"Good morning. You must be excited," said the old man.

"More like nervous."

"So is your opponent, I'm sure."

"Well, he's not a first-timer like I am."

It was true. His opponent wasn't a veteran, but he wasn't a rookie, either. He'd been on the Tour for five years and had already won a few tournaments.

But the old man always seemed to see the bright side of things. "Don't forget that you have a three-shot lead."

"I know, I know." Robert wished he had a ten-stroke lead to overcome Sunday afternoon's pressure, the worst in the game. But at the same time, it was the thrill every player was looking for.

"I suppose we should get going," Robert said to the old man after breakfast.

"I suggest we wait a little bit. It's only seven o'clock. Our tee time isn't until 12:05."

That was true. Being the leader, Robert was in the final twosome.

"Just sit back and relax," suggested the old man. "Try to picture every shot you'll play, hole by hole. Don't let any dark states of the golfer affect you. You're going to win today. You're really going to win."

How can he be so sure? wondered Robert. But then he thought, I cannot let him down. I cannot disappoint him. This is the man who handed me a twenty-five thousand dollar check without questions or a written contract, just a handshake.

Twenty-five thousand dollars. It would be easy to pay him back if he won the title. First prize was four hundred fifty thousand dollars! But what if he choked and played a disastrous last round, shooting 78, or, even worse, 80? Then he would end up at the twenty-fifth or thirtieth slot and collect ten thousand dollars at the most.

There were so many stories of unknown golfers who shared the lead for a few rounds then blew it and shot 82 on the final round. Playing golf was one thing, but handling pressure was another.

Robert went back to his room and lay down on his bed. Instead of picturing his final round shot by shot as the old man had suggested, he started thinking about Paul, who was not well at all. He did not want to disappoint him, either. He had to win for Paul . . . he had promised he would.

Then he thought about Clara. They had been separated for more than three months now. Still, he hoped they would get back together. The last time he spoke to her, she didn't say that it was over, but that she needed time. Time. Was it on his side now? What time was it, anyway? He glanced at the clock. Already eight o'clock! He jumped out of bed at the exact moment the millionaire knocked at his door.

"It's time to go, kid."

Great timing, thought Robert. I hope my timing is as good today.

Minutes later, he was sitting in the back seat of the limo with the old man and an unusual companion, Freddy the fox, who was dressed for success in an Irish-green vest that made him look adorable. Robert petted the fox for a little while, then his mind stated racing again. Clara . . .

He knew it was a bit early to call, especially on a Sunday morning, but Clara was usually up at seven, even on weekends. Robert really wanted to talk to her before the final round. At least for a few seconds. She had always believed in him, in his talent and worthiness. Just to hear her voice would help him, he was sure.

"May I use the phone?" Robert asked.

"Of course."

He dialed her number and the phone rang. When a man's voice answered, Robert quickly hung up, thinking he had dialed the wrong number. He dialed again, carefully pushing each button. It rang, and again he heard a male voice. He hung up, feeling shocked and devastated. Clara already had someone in her life—and he was living with her! That's why she said she needed more time!

"Something wrong?" the millionaire asked.

"No, no . . ." Robert would have liked to tell him why he was upset, but he felt too humiliated.

The old man smiled skeptically. "Calm down, kid. Calm down."

"I wish I could."

"Just do as Freddy does! He's not nervous. For him it's just another Sunday morning."

Distracted, Robert answered, "Well, Freddy Couples is Freddy Couples. He's won thirty tournaments. I haven't!"

The millionaire had a good laugh. "No, not Freddy Couples. Freddy the fox!" He scratched the dozing animal behind the ears. "Freddy here doesn't care whether it's the U.S. Open final round or not. Neither should you. Just calm your mind and trust your instincts. Your putter doesn't know you're a first-timer—neither does your driver."

The drive to the golf course was very short since the U.S. Open was held in Long Island, not far from where the millionaire lived in the Hamptons. When they stepped out of the limo, the little fox seemed ready to come with them.

"No, Freddy, you wait for us in the car with Edgar."

Freddy sadly watched his master and Robert walk away. Then he noticed the window was half open. Edgar was busy navigating through a crowd of spectators who were trying to peer into the limo to see which golf celebrity might be inside. Perfect! Freddy jumped out of the window, but his master and Robert were nowhere to be seen. He had lost them in the crowd.

* * *

As Robert approached the first tee, he was so nervous he could hear his heart pounding. Things were even worse when he saw the crowd waiting for him, at least five hundred spectators wanting to see the underdog everybody was talking about and how he would handle Sunday's pressure.

"Robert Who?" asked a headline in the morning paper.

Everybody wanted to know. Robert, too, in a way. He would certainly find out very soon what kind of a man he was.

The first hole was a long and narrow par four rated as the third-toughest hole on the course. Every player had a choice to make for the tee shot—driver or iron. An iron was more precise, of course, but then you'd end up with a much longer second shot to a narrow and well-protected green. A driver would give you those extra yards, but a drive in the rough— U.S. Open rough—would also mean a difficult second shot, and maybe a bogey, nothing to build up your confidence on the first hole.

Robert's playing partner decided to go for the driver. He wanted to make a statement. He was three shots back, no time to play it safe. The crowd loved it. He quickly smacked a 280-yard drive right down the middle.

In his game plan Robert wanted to start with a one-iron. But he thought he would look like a loser and changed his mind.

"Driver, please," he asked his caddie.

The old man picked out the club and handed it to him.

Robert hesitated then said, "No, give me a one-iron instead."

The millionaire showed no emotion as he handed him the iron.

Robert took his stance and swung. But he pulled his tee shot and ended up in the left rough. "I knew it," he muttered. "You want to play it safe, but you miss it anyway!"

"Calm down," said the millionaire when they got to his ball. "It's only the first hole. And look, you have a fairly decent lie."

That was true. The ball was sitting well. He could make clean contact with it. The only problem would be to stop it on a small and fast green.

"It's just a long par three," said the millionaire.

Robert hit a perfect four-iron and managed to stop the ball, then two-putted to salvage a par that felt like a birdie.

"Told you!" said the old man. "You should listen to me more often."

Robert smiled with relief. His adversary had missed a long birdie putt. He was still three shots ahead.

But Robert lost his lead after three more holes, missing two short par-saving putts while his opponent sank a fifteen footer for a birdie.

"That's it, I'm dead," Robert thought.

But on the next hole he made a forty-foot birdie putt and his confidence was back—even if his playing partner also birdied the hole. Your own confidence will never stop your opponent from playing well. Indeed, his rival chipped in on the ninth hole, an unlikely eagle even on a short par four.

"Now I'm really dead!" Robert groaned.

"And if you'd like, you can choose your coffin right away," said the old man, talking like a second-rate salesman. "We have a large variety of colors and prices!"

Robert couldn't help but laugh. For a second the situation didn't seem so dramatic. But he was still nervous. He was trailing by two and had a demanding afternoon ahead of him.

"There are still nine holes to go," said the millionaire.

"Yes, I know."

The tenth hole was a relatively short par five that most players could reach in two. Robert's opponent hit a nice tee shot, but Robert really flushed his drive, well over three hundred yards, dead center.

"Way to go!" cheered the old man. "The coffin will have to wait."

His partner, who had hit first, reached the green in two. Robert selected a five-iron but hit it fat, and the ball fell short of the green on the left side in the rough. The crowd let out a huge "Oh!" Now he was in trouble! The underdog could not stand the pressure. He was two shots down and his opponent was already on the green with a very make-able eagle putt.

He was dead. Robert noticed a smile on the other player's face that seemed to say You're choking. You're running out of luck.

Robert felt discouraged. But then he told himself, Stop thinking. Stop thinking. One shot at a time. Don't let the dark states of the golfer invade you.

When he saw the lie of his ball, he felt he could make a decent shot. Get close to the pin and make birdie. He studied the situation. He had a bunker to cross to reach the green, which was narrow and sloped downhill past the flag.

"What should I do?" he asked the old man. "If I hit short, I end up in the bunker. If I hit long, the ball might as well roll off the green."

"No time to think about all the 'ifs.' Just hit the perfect shot," the millionaire said crisply.

"The perfect shot?"

"Yes, the shot you need."

"What I need is to sink the damn ball!"

"That's what I meant. Sink it!"

"You think I can do that?"

"You have to. Just see it flying in the air, very high, just two feet past the bunker and rolling smoothly into the hole."

Robert looked at the old man. He was absolutely serious. He had no doubts in his mind.

"I know you can do it," said the old man. "I know you can do it. Think of nothing else. Just see the ball rolling into the hole."

"Easier said than done!" Robert thought. Then he told himself, "I will do as I am told."

He took his stance, made a few practice swings, trying to picture the perfect shot. Finally, he hit his shot. He made good contact and the ball popped high in the air. So high, in fact, that Robert thought, "Shit! I overcooked it. It'll end up in the bunker."

He was wrong. The ball landed exactly where the millionaire had wanted it to land, two feet past the sand trap, then it started rolling toward the flag, picking up speed quickly.

"Damn," thought Robert. "I'll have to chip again."

He was wrong again. The ball hit the pin and disappeared into the cup! Eagle three!

The crowd let out a huge roar. He hadn't choked on that one!

Robert cracked a big smile and made a fist.

"Well done, kid! Well done!" the old man congratulated him. "Now keep your cool."

"I will."

His opponent did not. He was so rattled by the miraculous chip shot that he three-putted. Robert was back in the game as a co-leader. The next three holes, Robert was on a roll and made three birdies in a row while his partner had to work hard to save pars. Now Robert was leading by three.

But on his way to the fourteenth hole tee off, a spectator shouted at him, "You loser! You'll never make it."

Suddenly, Robert's confidence vanished.

"Don't listen to him," the millionaire said.

"I won't."

But he did, because he made mistake after mistake. On the seventeenth hole he missed an easy uphill two-footer to save par, bringing him back into a tie with his competitor. The momentum was now on his opponent's side. So there he was, Sunday afternoon of the U.S. Open, co-leader. The champion of the tournament would be the man who won the next hole.

Losing a three-stroke lead and missing an uphill two-footer could shake the confidence of the most experienced player. As a matter of fact, Robert was so nervous that he could feel the pulse in his eyeballs. It got so strong that his vision blurred.

The eighteenth hole was a short par five under five hundred yards. But there was more than one catch—a water hazard just in front of the green, deceiving winds blowing in from the ocean, and trees bordering the fairway. All week long players had made bad judgments and ended up in the water, making it difficult to save par.

Robert's opponent, who seemed so poised, teed off first. He hit a perfect drive two hundred and seventy yards down the middle. The gallery oohed and aahed, breaking into wild applause as the ball bounced to a stop.

A silence fell as Robert set his ball on the tee. He took a few practice swings and started thinking, I mustn't drive it into the trees. I absolutely must not hit the ball into the trees. If I hit the ball into the trees, I'm dead . . . It took a moment before he realized he was making a mistake. He chased the negative thoughts from his mind, picked out a target in the middle of the fairway, a distant point, and concentrated. His heart was beating so fast it felt like it would burst out of his chest. He could almost hear it. The pressure was incredible. He had to calm down. There was no way he could make his shot in such a state.

He took a few deep breaths, trying to detach himself from the situation. There weren't hundreds of spectators watching his every move. This wasn't the last hole of the U.S. Open, with him tied for the lead. He didn't have to hit an exceptional drive down a narrow fairway bordered by forest on both sides. He was all alone on the driving range. He was going to hit a number-one wood, just like the thousands he'd hit before, smoothly, without forcing, perfectly calm.

He did not. He overswung and pushed it into the woods. He could not believe it. The shot was a disaster. His ball was somewhere in the trees. If he couldn't find it, he'd be penalized two shots. The tournament would be over for him.

He glanced over at the millionaire. For the first time since their meeting, he caught the old man looking surprised, as if events had for once surpassed him, even though he showed no outward sign of agitation.

"We have to find the ball," the old man said, as if nothing else mattered. "So let's go find it."

The two men walked quickly and soon reached the stand of tall pines. A number of people were already looking for the ball, which could have been anywhere in a fifty-yard radius.

Meanwhile, his opponent, who was up, put his ball on the green. After searching in vain for some minutes, Robert knew he was beat. He would finish the tournament in disgrace. He might as well head back to the tee, hit another halfhearted drive and hope he wouldn't drop too far down in the standings, so at least he'd come out with a decent-sized check. Small consolation for a man who just moments before was on the verge of becoming a champion, of winning the U.S. Open title.

He was about to head back when he noticed Freddy the fox sitting quietly in a small clearing, just like the day he'd first seen him on the millionaire's course. He walked closer, feeling a shiver run down his spine. Freddy stood up. There, between his front paws, was a golf ball. Robert hurried closer and took a good look at the ball. Yes! It was his! Thank you, Freddy! Thank you!

Robert hollered for a judge, then looked around. Not only was it his ball but he also had a clear shot out of the trees. It was a very slim chance—it would take the best shot he'd ever made in his life to get close enough to the green to remain in contention. But it was still a chance.

He winked at Freddy, who ran off as soon as the judges came clumping through the trees.

The millionaire joined Robert, beaming.

"Lucky for us Freddy was around," Robert said.

"I don't know how he did it. We left him in the limo with Edgar."

Now all Robert had to do was play the shot. He was about two hundred yards from the flag. He had to hit a perfect four-iron very high in order to avoid the water and stop almost immediately on the green. Not an easy shot.

"Take your time," the millionaire said. "Don't do anything until you're ready."

Robert did take his time. He knew that once again he needed the perfect shot, but this one was even more difficult than the earlier chip shot. This time, if he missed, he'd stay in the woods or end up in the water and he'd lose the title. It took a little while, but then he saw it. The perfect shot. And he had the feeling he could hit it and win, even if the odds were against him with his opponent already on the green in two with a very makeable eagle putt from eighteen feet and a sure birdie.

Yes, the odds were against him, but Robert truly believed he could pull a perfect shot. He did not wait long, took a deep breath, and swung. The ball almost hit the top of the trees in front of him but flew nicely to the green, where it landed and stopped, only three feet from the hole. An amazing shot. The crowd exploded. The underdog had pulled another beauty—in fact, an almost impossible shot.

For the second time in the round, Robert smiled broadly.

"You did it! You hit the perfect shot!" the old man slapped Robert on the back.

But as they say, it's not over till it's over.

The other player was on the green sizing up his putt. If he made his putt, Robert would have to sink his to send the game into a sudden death playoff. And the odds were against him, because first-timers rarely performed well in sudden death.

A few seconds later, his opponent's ball was rolling toward the cup. When it was a foot away, Robert realized it was going in. It was heading straight for the hole. It was all over—there was no way Robert could withstand the pressure in sudden death. At the last instant, however, the ball seemed to hit a tiny bump in the cropped grass. It shifted slightly toward the right, caught the edge of the cup, came to a stop, but did not fall in. A sigh of incredulity rippled through the packed gallery. Robert could not believe it. It was like God granting him a reprieve from a death sentence. His opponent made a sour face as he tapped the ball into the cup, then stepped to the edge of the green, shaking his head in dismay, impatient to see how Robert would fare. Would he be able to sink the short but deceptively difficult putt? Or would he choke again, as he had on his tee shot?

Robert was well aware that the winds of fortune had shifted in his favor. This was his chance to win. He took his time, examining the putt from every angle. All he had to do was make a putt. Only one putt to become the U.S. Open champion—and pocket four hundred fifty thousand dollars!

When he was satisfied with his analysis of the green, he got into his stance. As he stared from ball to cup, drawing the line the ball would take in his mind, he found it strange that it had all come down to this—a three-foot putt just like the ones the millionaire had made him shoot on the practice green, increasing the stakes for every shot, betting first a thousand, then ten thousand, then a hundred thousand dollars. An amazing coincidence? Fate? Some mysterious law of cause and effect? He could not say. All he knew was that he had to make this putt. And yet, he remembered how he had been too nervous to shoot the hundred-thousand-dollar putt on the practice green. He had frozen up. Would the same thing happen now?

He took another good look at the line between ball and cup, made sure his putter was perfectly balanced in his hands, and was just about to make the shot when he hesitated. He needed more time. The green was fast. There was the curve to worry about. Had he taken the grain of the grass into account?

He couldn't start lining up the shot all over again, not in front of all these people, not in front of the TV cameras, with millions of viewers watching around the world. He'd look like a complete idiot!

Suddenly things started spinning around in his head. He was losing control. He felt his heart racing faster and faster; every beat made him more convinced that he was going to miss. Missing short putts in crucial situations had been a trademark of his game before he met the millionaire. He was a past master at muffing decisive shots! What the hell, he thought, get it over with. You can't put it off forever!

His putter head swung back, then forward, made contact with the ball. It rolled, swerved to the left, and stopped a foot from the hole. Robert squeezed his eyes shut. When he opened them he saw his ball still in front of him. He'd been hallucinating!

He made a supreme effort to regain control. He visualized the ball making a perfect curve and disappearing into the cup, took a final deep breath, and made his shot.

He closed his eyes again. He couldn't bear to watch. He prayed silently, knowing that his entire future depended on this one simple putt. After what seemed like an eternity, as if time were standing still, he heard a sound, a little insignificant sound, but the sweetest sound a golfer could ever hope to hear—the *plop* of his ball falling into the cup. The crowd roared. Robert opened his eyes. It would not have surprised him to find that he was dreaming again, that he hadn't made the shot, that everyone was still waiting.

But his ball was nowhere to be seen. It wasn't on the grass in front of him and it wasn't anywhere near the hole.

He took a step forward and then he saw it, immobile, white as perfection, at the bottom of the cup. He scooped it out, kissed it, and threw it into the crowd. The millionaire rushed over, threw his arms around his protégé, and pounded him on the back.

"I'm proud of you, boy! I'm so proud! I knew you could do it! I knew it!"

For the first time Robert saw tears in the old man's eyes. A whirlwind of emotion burst inside him. It was too much—too much joy and relief for one heart to contain. He felt tears running down his own cheeks.

"I'd never lend someone twenty-five thousand dollars if I wasn't sure I'd get it back!" the millionaire joked, trying to lighten things up.

Robert's opponent came up and shook Robert's hand warmly. "You did great. Welcome to the club!"

For a second Robert wondered what club he meant. Then he realized—the club of champions! He'd won the U.S. Open!

"Robert! Robert!"

He heard a voice in the crowd. A voice he knew. He stopped walking, turned around, and saw somebody he was not expecting.

"Dad?" Robert stammered.

"Congratulations, son."

Fresh tears came to Robert's eyes. It was the first time in his life that his father had said that to him.

"We're so proud of you, Bobby," said his mother. She clasped her son in her arms. Robert felt he could have stayed in those arms forever, but TV cameras were closing in, reporters were clamoring for a word from the U.S. Open champion. There would be time for tender reunions later.

The Cup was presented with the usual pomp and cere-mony. Robert kissed its cold surface, then held it over his head as the cameras clicked and flashed. He was handed a check for four hundred fifty thousand dollars, more than he'd made in five years as a golf pro back at his old club. Not bad for a day's work, not bad at all!

As he stood there beaming for the photographers, he caught sight of the last person in the world he expected to see—Clara, accompanied by a man he didn't know.

Doing his best to conceal his emotion, he signaled her over. She pushed her way through the throng of journalists until they stood face to face.

"Robert, congratulations!" she smiled warmly, then turned to the man by her side. "This is my cousin George from L.A. He's visiting for a few days."

"Oh, pleased to meet you," Robert said, really meaning it. So Clara didn't have a new lover, only a visitor.

"I, um, I saw your picture in the paper," she said. "I've been around for a couple days actually, but you were concentrat-ing so hard, I guess you didn't see me."

He didn't know what to say, didn't know if he should just take her in his arms and kiss her, which is what he felt like doing. All he knew was that he loved her, that he had never stopped loving her.

He could see in her eyes that she loved him, too. Maybe, just maybe, they could work things out, start over. All that love made him think of the one person he had done all this for, the person who had believed in him the most: Paul. He had to take the trophy to the hospital and share his victory with the boy.

George, who could clearly read the unspoken dialogue taking place, grinned and excused himself, saying he'd see Clara back at the house.

"Come on," Robert said, taking Clara by the hand, "there's someone we have to see."

The millionaire was waiting in his limo. Seated beside him in the back seat was Freddy the fox, looking contented as the millionaire rubbed him between his soft ears. Robert introduced Clara, and they headed off to the hospital.

The news they got when they arrived was not good: Paul had suffered a relapse. Doctors and nurses hovered around the sickroom. But when the boy saw Robert, his face lit up with joy.

"You were awesome, dude! I knew you'd win!"

Robert laid the trophy on the bed beside him. As Paul ran a hand over its gleaming surface, his smile faded.

"What's the matter, Paul? What is it?" Robert said, trying to hide his concern.

"Now I'll never get to play with you," the boy whispered.

"What do you mean? Just because I won the U.S. Open doesn't mean I won't have time to shoot a few rounds with my best buddy!"

"No, it's not that. I'm going to die soon."

"What are you talking about?"

"I know I will. But it doesn't matter, I'm ready. Last night I dreamed an angel came to see me. He told me I'd be coming back soon after I died, that I'd get to see my parents again. I'm happy about that. But you have to promise me one thing. When they come back from vacation, tell them not to worry. Tell them I'm dead but I'll be coming back. All they have to do is . . . is love each other . . ."

"I'll tell them, I promise," Robert said, fighting back tears. Freddy, who had somehow gotten into the room without being noticed, jumped up on the bed and licked the boy's face.

"Freddy! You came! Hey, boy!"

Paul hugged the animal to him and closed his eyes, happy as a boy could be. A nurse glanced at the sickbed and shrieked. Blood was trickling out of Paul's mouth, and the nurse thought he had been bitten. She rushed over to grab the animal, but quickly realized her mistake. Paul was spitting up his own blood. She shouted for a doctor, but it was too late. Paul was dead.

16

In Which the Golfer and the Millionaire Go Their Separate Ways

SHAKEN AND TEARFUL, Robert and Clara were invited to spend the night at the millionaire's residence. Over dinner, the millionaire began philosophising about death. "I know it's hard to lose someone you love. I remember when I lost my beloved wife, I greived for months. But then I remembered that death is nothing but an illusion. We are the soul, not the body. And the soul is immortal. The body is like the car we drive. Are you still sad because you lost your old Riviera in an accident?"

"Of course not. But Paul was so young . . . I'll miss him. I'll miss his charm, his faith in me."

"Maybe he'll come back," said the millionaire.

"How can you say that?" asked Robert.

"We do not come to earth only once. We come many, many times. And most of the time in the same family, with the same friends."

"It's possible," said Clara. "I've read that we always come back to the ones we love." She smiled at Robert.

"And to the ones with whom we have conflict," added the old man. "That's why we have to be careful until we learn the lesson we're supposed to learn, which is a simple but difficult one: To love each other perfectly. And then we are free at last."

* * *

The next morning, before leaving with Clara, Robert handed the millionaire a check for the money he owed him. He also gave back the keys to the Ferrari.

"Keep it," the millionaire said.

Robert stared at the old man. "Are you kidding?"

"That car never belonged to me anyway. When I bought it, I felt like I was buying it for someone else. Now I know who."

"I . . . I don't know what to say."

"So don't say anything! All I ask in return is that you be yourself. That's the hardest thing I can ask of anyone. Try to be at peace with yourself in everything you do. Share what I have taught you with others. Through words, of course, but more importantly through deeds. Set an example. That's the best way to teach. Become a great golfer, and above all, become a happy man. In this day and age, that's the best you can do if you really want to help people. If you're unhappy, you can't help anyone. The reason we're here is to grow, to evolve by helping others."

The millionaire fell silent. Robert knew it was time to go. Henry the butler came running down the steps balancing a cellular phone on a silver tray.

"It's the President, sir," Henry puffed.

"Tell him to hold," the millionaire said. Robert walked up to the old man and took him in his arms, hugging him like a father. The millionaire watched serenely as Robert and Clara climbed into the Ferrari, then turned his attention to the phone call from the President.

Robert was about to put the car in gear when Freddy the fox came trotting out of the bushes. Robert whistled and the animal came over for a last scratch behind the ears.

"I almost forgot about you, didn't I, boy?" Robert said. "Yes I did. Almost forgot to thank you, didn't I?"

Freddy licked his hand in farewell and went gamboling off into the rose garden. As he drove down the driveway toward the front gates, Robert turned to Clara. "Do dreams come true? What do you think?" he asked.

Clara seemed to read his mind.

"You're wondering if Paul is really going to come back, aren't you?"

"Well? Do people come back?"

"I don't know. I really don't know."

"How about if we try and bring him back? Tonight."

"What do you mean, like some kind of ritual?"

"Yeah, a kind of ritual . . ."

He reached over and placed a hand on her belly. She felt the warmth of his palm and understood. That evening they would make love, passionate, affectionate love. Nine months later a child would be born, a boy they would name Paul. They would never know if it was the same Paul, but they might indulge themselves and believe it was.

Would they be wrong?

Hard to say. Faith is a powerful thing.

About the Author

Mark Fisher is the bestselling author of *The Instant Millionaire*, which has had phenomenal success since its publication in 1989—selling more than 150,000 copies in the United States alone and translated into 21 languages. A full-time author and enthusiastic golfer, Mark lives in Montreal with his wife and daughters.